P

A painstaking, persona[...]
vivors and trans women and anyone dreaming and yearning on the margins. *Faltas* is as intentional, resilient, original and acerbic as its activist author.

— **Janet Mock**, *author of* Redefining Realness *and* Surpassing Certainty

Cecilia Gentili is a brilliant writer whose *Faltas* (Spanish for "errors") are infallible reports from the front lines of trans literature. She has so much courage and grit and is outrageously daring. The villains and saints in her childhood and adolescence she evokes with truth and humour. This book is irresistible!

— **Edmund White**, *author of* A Boy's Own Story *and* A Previous Life

Cecilia Gentili is a born storyteller—her voice jumps from every page. Her humor and warmth disarm you before sudden turns into the shocking and accusatory. *Faltas* pulsates with the same thrill as listening in secretly to a phone call, opening someone else's mail, reading a strangers' diary. You know it's wrong but you'd do anything to keep going.

— **Morgan M Page**, *writer,* Framing Agnes

These are bewitching letters that do everything all at once: accuse, forgive, mock, heal, teach, seduce; stories that transcend classification and reality even as they tell hard truths. Cecilia Gentili is a singular voice that you can't miss.

— **Torrey Peters**, *author of* Detransition, Baby

I don't know if I've ever read anything so emotionally honest and morally rigorous. She manages radical empathy without compromising her own emotional integrity ... It's funny and clear and vivid and painful and also so complex ... We need this book, I kept thinking as I read. Fuck all the college reading lists for Ethics 101. Just assign *Faltas*. It's funnier than Kant, and more realistic.

—*them*

[A] breathtaking addition to the canon of works about "messy trans lives." ... one of the best memoirs I've ever read.

—*Autostraddle*

"Raw, incandescent ... groundbreaking ... powerfully and necessary ... *Faltas* is not a redemptive book or a story of victoriously emerging from a traumatic past, but that's not its aim. It is [written] by a woman determined to tell the truth and resolve unfinished business.

—*Chicago Review of Books*

I may never finish processing this book. Gentili's writing is so raw without ever feeling unpolished, so personal and unflinching. It is a trans memoir that apologizes for nothing and refuses to make compromises for cisgender readers. Gentili's treatment of the trauma central to *Faltas* is unparalleled; nothing feels sensationalized but nothing is shied away from. A phenomenal, important book.

—**Gus Thompson**, *The Ivy Bookshop (Baltimore, MD)*

A little earthquake of a book … powerfully glides through abuse, sex work, forgiveness, friendship and class mobility … with a storied career and life, characteristic humour and an eye for a witty barb, Gentili has crafted a warm, thoughtful, piercing book.

— *Xtra*

A revelation … emotionally and ethically complex … a story of learning to work with what little power one has … an outstanding quality of *Faltas* is that it avoids melodrama and moralizing. What it depicts is not a fallen world but the ordinary state of things.

— **McKenzie Wark**, *Liber*

A uniquely intimate and powerful story of reclaiming and rebuilding from childhood trauma. This will be a tough read for many people, but Gentili rewards readers with a perspective on becoming your true self that is valuable for any identity.

— *Porter Square Books (Cambridge, MA)*

Faltas

letters to everyone in my hometown
who isn't my rapist

Cecilia Gentili

Published by LittlePuss Press LLC, Brooklyn NY
www.LittlePuss.net

Cover design by David Knowles
Edited by Cat Fitzpatrick

Library of Congress Cataloging-in-Publication Data is available

ISBN 978-1-7367168-2-3 (paperback)
978-1-7367168-3-0 (ebook)

10 9 8 7 6 5 4 3 2

This book is for Peter
who has been showing me for ten years
(and continues showing me every day)
that the idea that "love hurts"
is absolute bullshit

CONTENTS

ROSANNA   13

INÉS   45

ALEMANA   73

HELENA   91

JUAN PABLO   111

ABU   137

MAMI   155

DELIA   191

Faltas

Rosanna

DEAR ROSANNA,

I struggled, *Querida*, with calling you "Dear." Do I like you? I haven't seen you for years outside your Facebook posts, always missing your father. Well, not always. You post lots of animals. Dogs. Some posts about diabetes. And then a picture of your father, dandling a grandchild on his knee, or cooing at a baby, or singing. *Feliz cumple, Pa!* I don't like these posts, Rosanna, so perhaps I don't like you either. Did I like you when we were little? Perhaps even when we were sharing the same neighborhood and friends and culture, I didn't.

What I do recall is that I was never able to read you. I could never know what you were thinking. And this has always been my ability. I don't mean some childish fantasy of telepathic powers that let you see someone else's thoughts. I mean I have always been good at knowing what people were thinking. Not word for word, of course, but the overall feeling. When Helena looked at someone's new shoes? She was envious and wished they would get scratched right away. When Doña Marchesi, the midwife, looked at Marcela Mio's slightly short skirt? She was thinking Marcela was already a whore, even if she was only 12. I knew that was what Doña Marchesi was thinking, and just to go one step further, I knew that she knew that I knew. She was good at reading people's thoughts too. We would lock eyes, silently telling each other, *I know*.

Doña Marchesi hated me. As long as I can remember she could see my thoughts, as I saw those of others, and she hated me for them. Had she hated me since I was born? She was the first person I ever laid eyes on: It was her who yanked me from my mother's womb. When my mother first told me this, I had a wild vision of Doña Marchesi pulling me out, umbilical cord still attached, and holding me up and glaring at me, instantly knowing I was trouble. I know she saw me as a devilish being. I wonder if she considered killing me right away, to save the world from having to contain everything I would become. That would have been a temptation for her.

She pulled her son away from me when I came on stage during the school nativity play. Do you remember that play, Rosanna? You were just a villager. Such an unremarkable role they gave you! I wanted, of course, to be cast as Mary, but I knew it would be a hard sell. The whole not-having-a-vagina thing. Nevertheless, I tried. There was even a moment when I thought I might pull it off. At the first rehearsal, they still hadn't picked a Mary, and I talked them into letting me fill in on a temporary basis, while they were deciding. As I put on Mary's white veil, I thought, *now they will see me, and they will realize this role simply cannot be played by anyone else*. Your father was there. He saw me playing Mary and smiled at me. But then Doña Marchesi intervened: She talked a whole bunch of shit about me, and they gave the role to Susana Jimenez.

This didn't bother me too much, though, because Susana was my friend. My rationale was: if Mary couldn't be mine, she should go to someone I liked. Susana fit the bill. The problem was, who was I going to be, if not Mary? Susana and I sat down and examined a postcard of the nativity. She asked me: Which of these do you like? We considered all the characters one by one. Or specifically, all the female characters and also Gabriel the Archangel.

There was an attractive theatrical aspect to Gabriel's costume. Additionally, he would either descend from heaven on ropes, or be perched on some sort of platform, floating over everyone else, either of which was desirable. The downside was, whoever played Gabriel would have to provide the technical means of elevation, and I knew my father wouldn't help.

And then, right in the front lower corner of the postcard, I saw them: the three kings! They were wearing long robes that looked like luxurious dresses! They were wearing jewelry, a lot of it! And one of them was wearing a turban! Perfection!

I knew that if I showed interest, Doña Marchesi would make them give it to someone else, so I formed a plan. None of the boys would choose to be the kings—they were too feminine. So what I would do was nothing. I wouldn't ask for them either. I would let those roles go unfilled. I would hold back until playing a king would be a favor I was doing.

I waited. And, while I waited, I started preparing everything. Then on December 21st, at the rehearsal, someone screamed, "We don't have the three kings!" And I rose, to save the day.

"I can do it," I said. "I don't have enough time to work on the costume, but I will put together whatever I can." They all thanked me. All except Doña Marchesi. She saw through my scam, but it was too late for her to do anything. She had to eat it. She looked at me and her eyes were singing: *I know what you are doing, little bitch*. I looked the other way, then rushed home to add more rhinestones to my turban.

The day of the nativity scene, I was even glad I hadn't got Mary. So boring, all in white. Instead, I made my great entrance, wearing a cape, with glitter all over. When Doña Marchesi saw me, she pulled her child away and I saw her talking to him right below the stage. I couldn't hear her words, but I knew she was telling him: "Don't go near that little devil or you will become like him." I knew that's what she was saying.

After that, I would try to get close to him on purpose, and watch him run to the other side of the room, or playground, or whatever. I can't lie, I liked being demonized. At least I was *something*. I was someone who would be remembered. Someone extraordinary, fierce! I loved attention, even if it was attention that caused most of the pain I suffered.

So, as I said, I always had a good sense of other people's thoughts. Not yours, though. You were one of those I could never figure out. Later in life, I figured out that those I couldn't read were usually either the most vicious or the most compassionate people. Which are you, I wonder? Life pulled us apart, and we had never really been close, so I never got to find out. Not that I care, not that it's some kind of "unfinished business," not that I really give a shit about your soul, Rosanna. It's only because I hate carelessness that I had a hard time calling you "Dear." I ask myself, how can I call you "dear" if you have never been dear to me? I should bring this to my next therapy session.

Yes, therapy. I should tell you that therapy has been fundamental in finding the courage to write this letter. I am sure it will take much more courage to send it: perhaps another 10 years of sitting in front of my therapist Jianna, putting up with her saying, "What I am hearing here is . . . " before she repeats what I just said, which she does every time I say something that shocks her. She thinks I don't know that she is shaken by some of the information I vomit up in our sessions. But as I told you: I know with most people, I know what they think. Jianna's not the exception. You are.

Getting to the point, Rosanna: Your father raped me.

It started at age 6 and it continued for years. He sexually abused me for the rest of my childhood and adolescence.

᠊ᢒ

Before moving into the neighborhood, my mother and I had lived in a very old home. Well, we didn't live in a home, we lived in a single big room with walls that were damp and without plaster. It had a very particular smell. I always thought it was the smell of poverty because Mami would perfume us heavily before leaving, saying "you smell like the house." Mami never thought she belonged there. Neither did I.

I am not saying I hated it. It just didn't feel like our habitat. Mami always led me to believe we were meant to be glorious and I fully bought it. Always.

Outside, there was a palm tree, which nowadays I question: Why was there a palm tree? We did not live in Caribbean weather. We had hot summers, sure, but a palm tree? So tall! I always wanted to climb it. During the day, when she was busy, Mom would sit me under the palm tree with a half watermelon and a spoon and the heat around me. I would eat so much that I would fall asleep with my legs open, holding in the middle the green bowl, now emptied of its rich pink insides. Eyes closed with the spoon still in my hand.

At night, we would sit under it together, looking at the stars. I mean, not always. But sometimes. Other times, depending on how Mom's pill had kicked in, we might go outside to meet with the neighbors, drinking beers and smoking cigarettes on the sidewalk. Although there was not really a difference between the street and the sidewalk, or the sidewalk and the floor of the house. It was all dirt. I guess those boundaries were imaginary.

The other possibility was that Mami would stay inside crying. So I loved it when she invited me out: If we were outside, it meant she was not just inconsolably sobbing in her bed. Instead we were under the palm tree, trying to identify stars and, more importantly, UFOs. Back then there was a whole craze about spaceships, which were spotted all over our area. So we tried to spot them too. You are a bit younger than me, but I'm sure you remember.

Where did we cook? I don't think we had a kitchen. It was everything together. Just a big room where we slept and cooked and dreamed. What I do know is there was no bathroom. We had to go out the back to use a rundown outhouse that smelled like—well, an outhouse. Mami would heat water and we would take showers in a big tin washing-up bowl, throwing the precious water over ourselves little by little with a cup, always eyeballing what was left because if you used too much too early you would have nothing to wash off the soap, and then you would itch during the night.

You might ask where my father was. We all did. Not loudly, since my mom was sensitive to the question.

Short answer: I don't think anybody knew. Some said he was doing business in the north, some said he was hiding from the military because he was a stern Peronista and they were looking for him to kill him. Whatever the reason, he just wasn't there. The cash he might have earned was not there either, nor, most importantly, the security and warmth a father brings to the home.

Even when he came back, later on, he just lacked all of that. Though he had shown up magically and unharmed out of nowhere, with no explanation given about his whereabouts for the previous couple years, he was still mostly no more than a body that slept and ate with us.

I think your dad knew that. I think he was very aware of the fact that Tito was not present, even when he eventually was. Not his money, not his protection. I think he was also very conscious of my mother's issues. And there was one other thing he knew: I was a girl. He understood my femininity as normal, and used that, too.

I remember the first time he laid eyes on me: I saw it, I saw he would give me that thing everyone else was denying me. He saw me as I was, and I didn't have to explain how I felt inside because for him it was visible.

He saw I was Cecilia. He saved my life and ruined it forever.

Life had been getting really hard for me at that moment. Questions were starting to come from everywhere. Questions about me. And your dad had an answer.

᠕

I always felt like an outsider. I had an extreme sense of not belonging to any group or place. I remember thinking that when I started school, then I would find a tribe. But at school, the other kids were very clear: *You are weird, you have no aptitudes for anything, and you can't hang out with us*. The only games I might have been good at playing were girls' games, and for some mysterious reason the girls would not allow me to do that, so it was mostly just me, playing by myself.

I don't want to sound like that was necessarily terrible. I loved going to school anyways. I was even happy that my family didn't have the money (yours didn't either, Rosanna) for the private school, "The Calvary." "The Calvary" was run by nuns, and somehow I always knew that the religious and I would not get along. Also, the children at Calvary had to wear pants for the boys or skirts for the girls, but at the local school we got a different uniform. Everyone, boys and girls, had to wear these little white tunics that were almost, dare I say it, angelic! When I put on one of these white outfits for the first time, I felt like I was wearing my first fully sanctioned dress.

Most of the boys wore trousers under it, but not me! Mami never dressed me, so I would put on little shorts, so short that when the tunic was over them you could not see them at all. I was basically wearing a short dress, showing off my legs, and I loved it. As you are aware, I have amazing legs. Your father loved my legs.

So beginning school, starting classes, was a hopeful and exciting time for me. After a couple of weeks, though, I went through a shocking awakening.

I always walked by myself all the way to school. It was a long way, but walking in a mini-dress was a treat! I remember that day I was also carrying a flower. A red carnation. I don't know why. Probably from the cemetery. We usually spent the weekends at my grandma's, and we'd go to the Baptist Church to see people being submerged in the water to be reborn with Jesus in their hearts (I was always afraid someone would drown and really get close to Jesus all of a sudden) and then after, we'd go to the cemetery to clean all our dead relatives' *tumbes* and put flowers on them. It was a very vibrant activity. So probably Mami had taken some flowers from the dead.

In any case, that day she gave me a red carnation to bring to the teacher. Which was unusual, but my mom was rarely usual, and I didn't question it. I was carrying the flower and my little briefcase. You had to have a briefcase to go to school, and they were all the same. There were no backpacks then, and I hated this briefcase because it wasn't feminine. If the tunics we wore made everyone a bit feminine, the briefcases made us all a bit masculine. Basically, it was ruining my outfit! It was a warm day and I walked all the way to school holding the flower and brief-case. I stopped to rest several times under trees so I wouldn't sweat and ruin my little dress before I made it to school.

As soon as I crossed the doorway, I saw the other children already lined up outside classrooms. Every day before class we had to form two lines, the girls against the wall and the boys next to them. Each line had to run from short to tall, and we had to stretch our right arms out, so as to almost touch the shoulder of the kid in front of us. I was late (too many stops under trees!) and I would have to break the line up. I hurried over, but then one of the secretaries called out my name. Caught! Clearly, I thought, I was going to be reprimanded.

I decided to play dumb, and I sweetly asked the secretary why she was stopping me. But she didn't reprimand me. Instead, she told me to go to the principal's office. This was much worse! It was only the second week of school, but it was already clear that if you got called to the principal's office then it meant some shit went wrong. So technically this was a scary announcement. On the other hand, that was already my specialty, dealing with shit going wrong. So I didn't let the secretary see me flinch. I just turned and sashayed off down the hallway.

I can still clearly see the hallways of School 290. Such a beautiful building. All the classrooms arranged around a breathtaking courtyard full of roses, open to the sky, where we would all start the day chanting to the Argentinian flag. Oh, the windows! The light! I walked towards whatever lay ahead through public splendor.

The hand in which I was holding the flower, my left hand, was sweaty, not from nervousness (though I was nervous) but because it had been clasping the flower for so long. I couldn't change hands, though: at that time I had a compulsion to only hold my hated little briefcase with my right hand, so the flower had to be in the left. This was just the beginning of my obsession with symmetry, one of many things in my life that only got worse through the years.

I walked to the office and the receptionist was waiting for me. She helped me open the thick wooden door. When it was fully open I gasped. Mami was there. My first thought was that she was giving me up to another family. I felt relief and sadness at the same time. I loved her, but I already knew at that age we were not a good match. I hoped they would send me to a rich family. I didn't care if they were bad people, just as long as they were rich!

Mami was sitting next to the principal, and next to her was Senorita Mabel, my teacher. I wondered if I should give her the carnation, but this didn't seem the right moment. Poised on each side of this central trio were two more women, making five of them in total.

The principal told me that these other two women were a psychiatrist and a psychologist.

They were all smiling and acting nice except for Mami, who was already crying. I began to realize I wasn't being given away.

The principal got up and walked behind the line of women, leaving her seat empty. There was something hanging on one of the walls, one of those pieces of fabric with a map or something on it that you could pull down or roll up. She pulled it down. It did have a map on it, but over the map they had stuck two drawings.

Perhaps, I pondered, there had been another restructuring of the country, since the army had taken over the government, and it was going to be explained to me that we now lived in a different province. I looked at the drawings. They were weird; I couldn't understand them at all.

As an adult, now, I see them clearly, and I know what they were intended to schematize. But at the time I was only five or six. I had no idea what I was supposed to be seeing. So they had to explain them to me.

They told me that one was a penis and that the other one was a vagina. I nodded, pretending I understood.

Then, the psychologist on the left stood up and walked over, slowly, and squatted down in front of me. Her ass almost touched the floor. She gently tapped herself between the legs and told me: "This is where these parts are. I have that one, the vagina."

Then she stood back up. What I had now learnt was her vagina hovered right in front of my face. For a moment I got distracted and looked down at her high heels. They were beautiful, patent leather, shiny and black, with her wide pants draping stylishly over them. Then I raised my head. My eyes travelled up, over her vagina area, all the way to her face.

She smiled again and pointed to one of the pictures pinned on the maps unrolled behind the line of women. It looked like one of the half watermelons Mami opened up for me, with a spoon on either side. She repeated the word, pronouncing it syllable by syllable. *VA. GI. NA.*

I frowned. She slowly walked around and stood behind me. I bent my knees and let my briefcase rest on the floor. Now my left hand was free! I switched the flower over into it, and uncurled my sweaty right palm. The psychologist touched my shoulder gently with her left hand, and pointed to the other drawing with her right. She said, "That is a penis. Unlike my vagina, it comes out of the body."

I looked at her and said: "Aaaaaahhhhh." Then I looked at Mami. She was still crying, making a soft noise. All her tears were collecting in the pool of her frenulum, above her half-open lips, and mixing with the soft clear mucus dribbling from her nose.

The principal must have followed my gaze, because she turned away from the map, hurried over to her purse, and pulled out a small handkerchief embroidered with lace. She offered it to Mami, who took it, but instead of blowing her nose she just patted at it, in total denial of the sheer amount of fluid coming from her face.

Meanwhile, the psychiatrist was behaving strangely. She almost stood up, stopped herself before becoming fully upright, crossed one of her legs under the other, folded it below her butt, sat back down again, and took hold of the hem of her skirt. I could hear the sound of her acrylic pantyhose rubbing together. I thought for a second she was going show me what she had between her legs. Instead she carefully pulled her skirt down over her knees, gently gestured at the pictures, and asked me: "What do you have?"

Was this a trick question? Although I was aware that historically I had had much better results from lying than the truth, I had a feeling I wouldn't get away with that here. But I was also unsure. What *did* I have? I thought for a minute and looked at the figures. I even took a step back, thinking perhaps if I got some extra distance, things would shape up differently. But they stayed the same.

I would have to come clean. After all, I reasoned, Mami had seen me bathing in the big zinc washtub with side handles we used as a bath. She would bring me boiling water to make the cold water we got from the manual well pump warmer and more enjoyable. I had seen her peeking at my body under the water. She, at least, definitely knew what I had.

I took a long breath and without looking at any of them I signaled the penis and said, "I believe it looks more like that one, but I could be wrong . . . "

The psychologist, who was standing next to me, went down on her knees. I heard her bones touching the floor and I looked at her face, which at this point was right in front of mine, and for some reason I teared up. I was not scared, but somehow I knew a bad revelation was coming.

She said, "Don't cry, little one. You have a penis and that makes you a boy. Now, let me ask you, where do boys go to pee and poo?"

Where did boys go to pee and poo? I responded, "To the bathroom."

She smiled quickly and raised one of her eyebrows. "To which bathroom?"

"To the boys' bathroom," I whispered.

"So, then, let me ask you," she said, standing up and hitting her knees to remove any dirt she might have collected while she was down by my face, "Why don't you do just as they do? Why do you go to the girls' bathroom if you have a penis like the other boys?"

Here I want to boast a little, Rosanna. Mami would be angry with me if she read this. She has always hated it when I praise myself. But I have to tell you, Rosanna, I have always been fast. I have always been able to figure things out in a second. Just as I had realized moments before that I couldn't lie when they asked me what I had, a penis or a vagina—so I also realized immediately that at that point, on the contrary, lying was exactly what was required.

I wanted, of course, to tell them that I was not a boy, to tell them I was a girl, but I knew nothing good would come from that answer. I let the tears I had been holding in my eyes come out (I knew they would soften their view of my little self) and said, "I think I got confused. I just didn't know."

Then I put my little hands over my eyes to give myself time to think up my next move. And as I did so, I noticed the stem of the red flower. Perfect!

Quick as a flash, I ran over to my teacher, who was still sitting next to my mom, and extended my hand to her, offering the carnation. I said to her, "I am so sorry I did this. I didn't mean to cause trouble!"

Mami's crying became so loud she was kind of screaming. The principal's handkerchief was saturated. The teacher couldn't contain her tears, either. As she took the flower with one hand, she grabbed my chin with the other and said, "Don't worry, little one. Now you know. We can make this work from now on. Just remember: When it is time to pee, you already know where to go."

I pulled my mucus up back into my sinuses by sniffing hard. Why, I wondered, had no handkerchief been made available to me?

"Now, let's go together to class with the rest of the children, as they must be missing us!" the teacher said.

Mami hugged me and whispered into my ear, "We will talk about this when you get home."

I looked at her and ran the knuckle of my index finger right under her eye, taking care of her last tear. I whispered back to her, "No."

If this refusal surprised her, she didn't show it. She got up and composed herself and said, "Go with your teacher. I will finish this conversation with the professionals."

"Of course, Mami," I said. I took Senorita Mabel's hand. "Thank you. All of you!" I yelled as we left. They all smiled. I hated them. All of them. All those women. Mami included.

When I got home later that day, Mami had, as I anticipated, seen the justice of my position, and given up on her scheme of addressing the issue further. We acted as if the day had been uneventful.

◞

At the time this was happening, my dad had only very recently returned. This was when we were starting school, Rosanna; perhaps you remember. When he came back, he came with a Ford Falcon. This was the only really exciting part about it. It felt like such a contradiction, living in a hut and having a decent-looking car. I guess Mami knew that the car wouldn't last longer than anything else in Papi's life, so she decided to rub it in everyone's face before it was gone. She started insisting we take car trips whenever we could.

Which was why, that weekend, she announced we would go to my favorite place in life: Grandma's house, in San Martin de las Escobas. There, I was able to live out all my fantasies without anybody staring at me, with grandma, who was my accomplice in everything!

In a rare turn of events, Claudio, my brother, was not only invited, but also agreed to come. I can still picture us all on that trip. It may have been one of the only times I ever had a sense of normality as a child: Papi at the wheel, Mami next to him resting her hands on her lap, me and Claudio in the back looking like normal siblings who knew and liked each other, sticking our heads out the half-open windows, enjoying the wind hitting our faces. It's almost like we should have had a dog too. But Mami disliked mascots with a passion.

There were two little towns between Galvez and San Martin: Rigby and Belgrano. Outside Rigby, the dirt road crossed a railroad. I felt the unevenness of the wheels running over the hard rails, once then twice, quick bumps. Claudio turned to me, leant down on his side, brought his head close to mine. I assumed he was going to hit me, but instead he gently said, "Come closer, Butterfly." He always called me that. *Mariposa*. Which starts as *Maricón*, but doesn't really go all the way there. A very Argentinian thing to do with offensive words. We don't like to be too obvious. We like to harm people, but in subtler ways.

"Come closer," Claudio said, and I leaned in on my elbow, and he cupped his hands to his mouth, leant right up to my ear, and whispered, "Did you see that railroad?"

I moved back away from him. His whispering had given me a weird chill. I looked at him and said, "Yes, of course."

He softly replied, "That's where we found you."

Everything stopped. The noise of the car disappeared. It was like I was suspended inside a bubble, like John Travolta in that movie, *The Boy in The Bubble*. I hadn't seen it, because we had no money to go to the movies, but I had heard from the other kids. I knew that was what it was like. Claudio continued, "About five years ago . . . "

"You all found me there!" I blurted.

"Shhhh," he murmured. He put his index finger over his lips. "Mami don't like to talk about this."

This made sense. Mami didn't like to talk about anything.

I said, "Was I in a basket?" I was thinking of Grandma narrating to me the stories from the Bible where Moses is dropped in the river in a basket to save him from the bad guys looking to get rid of Jesus Christ.

He said, "No, no basket."

I asked, "Was I wrapped in a blanket?"

He looked at me and flapped his hands up in the air without raising his arms. "No, no blanket," he said firmly. "You were just lying naked, back there, and Mami decided to take you with us, and that's why you live with us, but you are not my brother. Don't cry. Mami don't want you to know, but I thought you should know this."

If he was telling the truth, this explained so much. I had always felt like I was not part of this family. But then, who were they anyway? Did Delia Marchesi know about all of this? Was that the reason she hated me so much? Was I some kind of new Moses? (Maybe I could separate a river?) I wanted to cry, but I couldn't. I had to think, and that was what I did for the rest of the drive. I even came to some conclusions.

When we made it to San Martin, surprising Grandma with our arrival, I couldn't run to her fast enough. I jumped up onto her torso and wrapped my legs around her big hips and she hugged me, but she was not really paying attention to me. Her focus was on the new automobile. So I said, "Grandma, I have to tell you something."

She stopped looking at the car. "What happened? Someone hit you?"

"No. It is much worse."

She put me down and started walking down the patio towards the tangerine tree.

Mami, a bit insulted that Grandma was now ignoring the car, yelled: "We have a car!"

Grandma rapidly looked back at her. "I'll check it out in a minute!" Then she looked at me and said, "What happened?"

I started crying. I blurted out, "I know. I know everything!"

We sat down on two plastic chairs, and I proceeded to tell her: "I am an extraterrestrial. Do you see all the spaceships being spotted in the sky around us? They are looking for me, Grandma. Claudio told me I was found by the railway, and I just found out in school that what I have makes me a boy, and I just couldn't tell them I am not. They would not understand because they are not like me! But I am from a planet where girls like me have peepees! The lady called it *penis*."

"What lady?" Grandma asked.

"The psychiatrist."

"Does your Mami know about this?" We both looked to check Mami couldn't overhear. She was showing the car to grandpa.

I breathed deep.

"She's with them, Grandma. She thinks like them. They got me in school and explained to me that I can't use the girls' bathroom and Claudio said I was found in Rigby and with all the UFOs around it just makes sense, Grandma. You are the only one I can tell this to!"

She took hold of me by my shoulders. I thought she was going to shake me, but I think she just wanted to make sure I was not going to be teleported away.

"I love you," she said. "That makes so much sense. I just don't know how to help you. Do you want us to wait for them tonight?"

"Yes, Grandma. I knew you would get it." I felt such relief. A relief, Rosanna, strangely similar to that I had already felt when I caught your father staring at me, when your father laid his eyes upon me. At those times, when your father was gazing at me, it felt like someone from my planet was also living on earth. He gave me permission to be.

I have read a lot about predators. It is such a cliché, Rosanna, but I don't know any other way to explain it to you. It was just like you see in an episode on the National Geographic Channel. There is a soft cute gazelle with her baby, eating grass. The young one walks away from the mother and the cheetah is right there, in the middle of some fucking large weeds. Camouflaged. Motionless. In a yoga plank pose. Rigid, still but so alive, with all this energy running through its inside. And you anticipate the carnage, the chaos, but for a while no one moves.

Now imagine that picture, but imagine everything else gets frozen except the young gazelle and the cheetah. Imagine that the young gazelle, as if hypnotized, skips over to the cheetah and allows it to devour her, happy about it, as if the feeling of the fangs ripping into her tender flesh was a painful enjoyment, as if it illuminated her even as it killed her. And imagine nobody around makes a single move. Just as if it was not happening. That is exactly how I felt all those years while your father used my body. I let him—as I was letting everyone else—dictate my life and my sadness.

ﺱ

Of course, school continued to be hard. I am sure you understand that. You and your brother, like your father, were fat, and that is a bit like being queer. *Uy*! What a fucking fight it is to be. Just be.

It is funny to me how in all the American teen movies, *Mean Girls* and that sort of film, there is this idea of the queer, the rebel, the goth, and the fat kid getting together in school: being made fun of and bonding through the misery inflicted on them by the cute skinny popular kids. Coming together as one in their pain, finding the courage to move on. We could have been like that, Rosanna. We could have been close, shared experiences. We weren't. I repulsed you. Even the fat kids hated me.

Because school was bad, I therefore took every opportunity to skip it. In a rare motherly effort, Mami told me that if I had to miss school, I should at least get the homework and do it. This was actually fine by me. I didn't hate studying. I hated being in a room with twenty other kids who spent every minute making fun of me, calling me names, ridiculing me, hitting me, and making me feel unwelcome, while the teachers did nothing. Actual *studying* I loved.

So I got into the habit, after one of my "sick" days, of going to the kid that lived the closest, to ask him about the homework. That kid was your brother.

How I envied him! He was able to use what should have made him an outcast to his benefit. He was fat, but that helped him become the best goalkeeper in school, and being the best goalkeeper made him popular, so then it was like he was not fat anymore: He was a popular sports guy. I, on the other hand, couldn't find a way to make faggotry relevant. Why was nobody able to see how fabulous I was? My world was amazing, they could have joined me in it, and instead they mocked it.

I took my notebook and walked around the corner to your house. My stomach was squirming. Your brother was never happy to have the queer kid turn up at his place. Maybe someone would see and think he was a fag, too. Why should he risk the reputation that he had worked so hard to build?

As much as I liked making people uncomfortable, I felt for him. I envied him, but not with an envy that was destructive. I wanted to be popular, but without having to put my body between a strong dude with a ball and a soccer goal. Why was his bravery celebrated and mine ridiculed?

It was also true that, as I went to your house, I felt a bit of a thrill of curiosity. I always like to see how other people live, as if I could get some sense of normalcy by assimilating the lives of others. We were not normal. I always knew it, but I was embarrassed to discuss it with others. *Does your mom cry? All the time? Does your dad come home late, very very late? Does your mom ask you to steal money from your dad? Did your brother move out of the house at age 7?* I couldn't ask any of my friends questions like these. One, because I didn't have real friends (I mean there was Susana, but she was unreliable, only my friend when it suited her) and two, because I knew it was truly just us, that nobody would understand. So instead, I made comparisons quietly, through observation.

More than this, though, going to your house was an opportunity to gain insight into the lives of one of the most famous people in Galvez. Your dad was a celebrity! His voice was the foundation of the celebrated group *Las Voces de Galvez*. They sang on the biggest stages in Argentina, and everyone knew them. I wondered why someone famous was living in affordable government housing until I learned that musical fame, in those days, didn't make any money. Nevertheless, going to your house was a peek into the lifestyles of the poor and famous!

So I was nervous. I rang the bell. The door opened—and it was your father. Such a tense moment. I don't know why it is that when going to someone's house, you always expect the mother to open the door. But it wasn't your mother.

As I told you, he and I had locked eyes before. I guess now we would say it "made me feel uncomfortable." But that isn't right. It didn't make me feel uncomfortable. Why was that? I have asked myself this so many times, tried to reason it out, and I have come to understand that it was because I already felt uncomfortable all the time. Everybody made me uncomfortable. Even my mother sometimes made me feel like she wished she had another child, not me.

I felt uncomfortable when my voice was not masculine and when I couldn't understand why that was a problem. I felt uncomfortable when I was constantly reminded that I should not gesticulate with my hands when talking. "It makes you look like a butterfly," my mother would say, "keep your hands clasped." I felt uncomfortable when it was made clear that I shouldn't look at men however I looked at them, because it was too flirtatious, because they'd turn round and say, "'What the fuck are you looking at, faggot?"

Discomfort was my normal, so when I saw the lust on your father, I wasn't any more uncomfortable than normal. But it was special. He was looking at me. The real me. Not this boy everyone wanted me to be. I felt a release from the pressure to perform to survive, and so I didn't see him as an attacker. I actually saw him as a protector. Someone that would protect this little girl. I thought that way for years. I thought I should focus on the fact that his look at me was lovely, and not on what came after.

Just FYI, Rosanna, he didn't fuck me the first time. He fingered me and asked me to suck his dick "as you do with a lollipop." For many years I thought that I liked it. I have now come to understand that I didn't like it. I needed it. I needed someone to see me. I needed someone to look at me as the girl I was, to have the experience of being someone who was normal. I needed it and he knew that. He gave me the only thing I could not get from anybody else. Not even the people who were supposed to love me the most. They didn't really see me. He did.

But what I needed was not just to be seen as a girl, but to be treated like one, and that he didn't do. He treated me like you treat a woman.

I wish I had the terminology and knowledge to talk about this with authority. The vocabulary to explain to you why it was wrong. Is this even necessary? As if anyone would have the smallest doubt that this was wrong. But I am sure you have such doubts. I did. For years I invited what he did to me, encouraged it. For years I thought that it was good. That it helped me.

Your father opened the door, and he looked at me, one of those looks of his, and he let me into your house. I told him I had come to get the homework assignment from his son's notes. I sat at the table while he went to get them, taking in every detail of your home. It looked beautiful. I envied your TV. I envied everything. That house looked like the house a family lived in. There was furniture and it indicated: *family*.

I think I fell into some kind of reverie, thinking of how my life would be if I lived in this home, if your parents were my parents. I would be happy, watching TV in your dad's lap, wearing a cute pink dress while your mom smiled at us from the kitchen, where she was preparing dinner.

Then suddenly I saw your brother's *carpeta*, his homework folder, coming down on the table in front of me, held by one of your father's hands, and at the same time, Rosanna, I felt his other hand on my back. And then your father began to rub my back. I got goosebumps. Why was he touching my back? Why was he caressing me like that? I didn't even need to ask him those questions. I think he perfectly knew everything I was thinking.

He stood over me and he said, "I know you like this. I know your dad is not giving you the love we dads have to give to our girls. But I am here to show you. If he is not able to make you feel loved, I will, my little girl."

He called me his "little girl"! You know when you put that last Lego in whatever shape you are making? Or add the last piece to a puzzle? That kind of satisfaction I had never had, and that is how I felt. Something completed me. Something was just perfect.

My grandma allowed me to act feminine, and never stopped me from girly things, but she never called me a girl. She did not have the vocabulary for it. She tried not to call me a boy, but she never called me a girl. Inés allowed me to wear all her jewelry, and Elena let me walk in her high heels, but they both reminded me that it was a treat they were letting me have. It was not a permanent thing.

Your father calling me a girl, though, was not a moment. It was forever.

He said you and your mom were going to come back soon, and that we had to maximize our time together because nobody could know he was doing this favor for me. He said if people knew it would shame my dad for not caring for me, and also it would make you jealous, Rosanna. That is what he said. I almost cried over his devoted solidarity and generosity.

For a minute I hated my dad. I had never had negative feelings against him. Even though he was absent for so long, even though I knew he had other women and that he did not help Mami in anything, even though he didn't care for me at all, even though I sometimes thought that he was so ashamed of me, as Mami was too at times, I never hated him. But when your father told me that was what dads do for their girls, I hated my dad.

I asked myself, does Papi not touch me like this because he doesn't see me as a girl, or because he doesn't care?

The day after, I confess, I wondered if these things your father was telling me could really be true, if this could really be normal. It couldn't be, I thought. Or maybe it was? But that day, during my first time with him, I didn't have time to think about what he told me.

He led me to the room. His room. It was not as clean as the rest of the house. He opened the door of a big armoire and pulled down some boxes and took out a little booklet. It was small and thin, maybe 12 or 14 pages. He gave it to me and said it would explain the things we would be doing together. He said he would bring me up to date with all the information my dad had failed to give me.

What text there was looked like Spanish, but I couldn't understand most of the words. I told him this. He said it was not important, that I could learn from the pictures. So I looked at them.

Suddenly my terrible experience in school, the mortifying session about penises and vaginas, made sense. This was how everything worked. The penis went in the vagina.

I pointed at a picture of a vagina and said to your father, "But I don't have this one." He put his finger in his mouth, then quickly ran his hand under my Adidas gym pants and put it in my ass. It hurt. I screamed.

He took his finger out and said, "We shouldn't go so fast. Go back to the first page."

I turned the pages back to an image of a Black woman with a guy's penis in her mouth. I asked, "Like this?"

He said, "Yes. Do it like a lollipop." And I did as he said.

I'm sorry I got so carried away with the description, Rosanna. I don't want to gross you out. I just need you to know that this happened and that I can't change it.

You may be asking yourself why I am doing this. Am I right? I just need to tell you.

It went on forever and it changed forms, but I had a sexual relationship with your dad until I moved to the US. I was so disgusted by it all the time, and I couldn't stop doing it. I think the only way to escape my need to keep getting your father's attention was to fly so many kilometers away, and across so many difficult borders, that I knew that coming back was impossible.

Part of me wonders if there was any other way, then, in Galvez, that I could have obtained that attention and love your father gave me. The most normal answer is through my parents, but of course that was impossible. I feel nauseated right now just thinking about it, but at the time, I needed what he gave me, what he kept on giving to me.

I wish I could tell you that I am doing this for a specific reason, that I am writing to you to ask you to do or say something. I know I am not writing to hurt you. I don't want that. I don't want you to pay for his sickness in any way. I do think I want you to change your mind about him, but part of me tells me you will not be able to do that either.

Perhaps you will see me as a liar. It would be so much more comfortable for you to traduce me as a liar than to recognize that your dad was a monster. Although I'm sure that you, deep down, already know. You must have known this for a long time, as your mother must have, too, but like everyone else that was around these events, none of you knew how to deal with it or even acknowledge it, and nobody gave a shit about me.

I think you have an opportunity to change that, but I don't expect you to. I know I am hurting you, and I wish I could say I care about you, but I don't right now: I care about me, and this is what I need to do. And if it causes pain, I can't help you and I cannot be responsible for it.

Good luck,

Cecilia

Inés

Ay Inés!

Was my father a good fuck? I guess he must have been: You were so into him. Though that's not what my mother said. In fact, Mami only had her first orgasm in her 60s. Not with him. Obviously.

Mami and I had this in common: When we were finally orgasming, we thought we were dying. Like, truly dying. Me with your nephew Alejandro, and her with this dude she met after dad passed. I remember her calling me after it happened. She went around and around for a long time until I said: "Mom, what's up? What you want to tell me? I know you do want to tell me something."

So she did. As she was talking I could picture myself, except when I went through it I was 10, and for her it was a little later in life.

Mami had met this dude a while before, but was too ashamed to tell me because he was married. She didn't want me to know she was thinking of doing to another woman what you had done to her. But she also thought it was time to get what she'd never had. Like she smelled the nut! So she went for it.

I feel almost strange, telling you this. Almost embarrassed. I think America has taught me to be ashamed to talk about parents and sex. Trying to fit better into American culture, I must have blocked out the memories of how we lived, all in one room with our parents having sex in front of us. But Mami was not American, so she told me all the details.

She said that while they were getting undressed, just staring at each other, she was afraid that his wife had followed him, that she was outside the house now, about to knock at the closed window and yell, "Whore, leave my husband alone!" As Mami had dreamt of doing to you and my father so many times. But she and this dude were very attracted to each other, and then he kissed her. She said the way he kissed her, she didn't know such a thing was possible.

(I too am a sucker for a kiss. I remember as a child telling your nephew Alejandro that if he didn't kiss me, he was getting no ass. Not only that, I had to feel that he was *willingly* kissing me. And you know, he did it. He loved fucking me so much that he put passion into his kiss, too. Just to get his dick inside me. But for Mami there was no pressure needed. This dude loved kissing too.)

She told me he went down on her. She felt like she'd become the main character of one of the Jackie Collins books she devoured. Before then, with my father, she had identified more as a Danielle Steel heroine. Not that she ever got the Danielle Steele treatment from my father either, though, not in her real life. It had been a virtual reality. But now she was going over to the dark side, the Jackie side. My father was gone and this handsome construction worker, younger than her—he wanted her, needed her, and she needed that. She needed to be desired, and his tongue on her clit started to . . . *uy!* . . . to get her places.

But it was a difficult process for her. She wanted to pay full attention to the feeling of something as human as her and yet foreign touching her body, but she also kept thinking that it was not yet a year since Dad had died. Apparently there is some kind of year rule.

This sounds crazy, but it's not the first I've heard of it, Inés. A year of mourning with no moaning. Needless to say, this only applies to women. No man is requested to wait any specific time to fuck someone else after his wife's passing. But for women, it's a year, minimum. Mami couldn't get that out of her head. Shame can do terrible things.

But then she thought, who made this rule? Who would make her accountable for the transgression? Was there a list? Would she be put in a black book? And then she felt this . . . tingling . . . in the end of her big toe . . . it was God. Maybe God had made the rule about waiting a year, and it was all true, and she would now be stained forever. The feeling was moving from the toe to her full foot. Both feet now had a warm sensation of some kind of soft electricity. Had Jackie mentioned this somewhere? She couldn't think of when, but God was there, in her head, and Jackie was fading from it.

Was Jackie God? No, if God was one of them, God was definitely Danielle.

God was punishing her. She didn't wait a year. Dad was still warm, even though she never got anything good from him, not even this simple but overwhelming little feeling of shocks she was getting from this dude, which at this point were moving through her lower leg. Nothing good at all.

At that moment, I remember thinking, *Mami, Papi gave you me and I am good*, but I didn't say anything. I didn't want to distract from her narrative. I could not recall ever hearing her talk with so much passion. About anything. I could feel it in her voice, almost crying while telling me this story.

She said at this point it became clear that the feeling coming from her toes and going through her body was death. God was taking her life for not waiting a year and also for sleeping with a married man.

I asked her, "Why is Inés not dead then, if she slept with Dad when he was married to you?"

She responded quickly: "Because she's evil, and Godly things don't apply to her!" And she went right back to the feeling, to the current moving inside her and how it would be the end for her. She said she thought of me.

A tear hung in my lower eyelid when she said that. But that was not important. I asked her, "What happened?"

She said: "It has a name. I heard of it before, but I thought it was a lie. I thought I was dying, but then I had an orgasm like are described in the books, and I want more of them. They are so good!"

So then I told her about me and your nephew, Alejandro. I told her, Inés, that I had had the exact same thought when, sitting over him, with his enormous dick inside me, he started touching me in the front, and it happened. The same shame, the same conviction that this could only be death, the same real-life Jackie Collins miracle.

Somehow life gave us an experience to share. I think it was that moment when my mother first truly saw me as an equal, as a woman. Mom and I had so many things in common and still the worst relationship as mother and daughter. Perhaps we should have been friends instead. Our lives became so intertwined after that confession. It felt terrible that it was through the phone and not holding hands.

But what I wonder, Inés (and this is why I asked you if my father was a good fuck), is: Was the reason my mother could never orgasm with my father because you put a spell on her?

⌒

Mami told me many times you were a witch. Not that you were visiting witches, asking for help, as she sometimes did, but that you were a witch yourself, actually doing *brujería*. As a kid I had all kinds of fantasies: you making potions, you conjuring forces, you enchanting a bone stolen from the cemetery to signify my parents' marriage and then shattering it into pieces.

I should tell you I have just moved in with my boyfriend. Right now I am working on throwing out his ex's shit to make space for my things. He didn't do a good job of erasing his ex's presence in the house before I arrived. I think he feels guilty for not fulfilling her dream of being a couple and living together forever, though from what he tells me (not that I believe him, I make it a principle not to believe men) they were very unhappy together. Like my mom and dad. Which I guess makes me you in this movie.

Anyway, as I was throwing all her shit out, I found three weird glass containers. Like marmalade jars but smaller. Each one had a little damp strangely colored piece of kitchen paper inside. I became afraid they were witchcraft, some kind of trap my boyfriend's ex had maliciously left behind for me. I told myself I shouldn't open them. But curiosity has always been my problem. Looking at these jars of possible witchcraft, I felt the same curiosity I felt when I used to look at your jewelry box, wanting to open it. So of course I opened the jars. And as I opened them, I thought of you, Inés.

I started remembering a day, back in Galvez, soon after my family moved to the government houses. The housing projects, Americans would say.

It was summer, around 10 am, and I was planning to do one of the things I enjoyed most, one of those rare things where my overwhelming faggotry was not an issue, where I could laugh with other children instead of being laughed at: I was going to chase *El Regador*, the sprinkler!

The government houses were far from the developed downtown, and our streets were dirt streets. During the summer, they would get very dry, and any cars would throw up dense clouds of dust. So, twice a day, a truck with a huge water tank in the back would come to wet the soil, and we would run behind it, getting wet and laughing and screaming. And it went so fast that no one had time to comment on me and my flaws. Everything was too urgent. We would anticipate the truck, then run with it until we had no more breath. And because the moment of breathlessness was different for everyone, and different every time, it was a collective activity that was also completely individual. It was perfect!

So, it was 10 am. I took my shoes off and opened the back door, the kitchen door that would bring me to the patio. As I came out, but before I turned out to the street, I saw you coming along the back alley on your bicycle. You had a job delivering papers and magazines to different houses. I knew this because you gave me porno magazines.

I will admit, it wasn't all your fault. Initially you offered me issues of a children's magazine, *Billiken*. I thought at first that my father was having a rare fatherly moment, actually buying something for me. Then I realized it was just another of your bribes, which made it less special. I also noticed that in your bicycle basket, along with children's magazines and fashion magazines, you had some items sealed in black plastic bags. I was curious, of course, but I didn't want to ask you, so I went to the only smart person I knew, my faggot friend Juan Pablo. He was a little younger than me, but he knew everything.

Juan Pablo told me they were porno magazines. I'd seen porno magazines by then. Juan Pablo was adamant I should get some off you. His theory was that porno magazines were the best way to lure cute boys into jerking off in front of you so you could see their dicks. I'm not sure if I was more interested in seeing dicks or in pleasing Juan Pablo, but I said I'd do it.

When I told you I was done with *Billiken*, and I wanted the magazines in the black plastic bags instead, I truly expected resistance from you. There was none. You just handed the pornos right over, and I handed them to Juan Pablo, and he got the boys, and we all went into the eucalyptus forest behind the town. The perfect equation!

So, as I say, I knew you delivered magazines, but it was not normal to see you here, in the government houses. The people in this neighborhood didn't have money for periodicals! Who, I wondered, besides me, was getting a magazine in this low-class craphole?

You rode up to my house and looked at me and raised your hand. I didn't wave back (I knew if I waved to you and Mami saw me I would be in trouble), but I was instantly overwhelmingly curious about where you were going. You rode towards me, and at the same time, on the other side, *El Regador* came into sight down the block.

What a pickle! I could turn to the left and get the most water possible all over my little body. Or I could turn to the right and follow you to see whose house you were going to.

So, I compromised. I ran left, to the front of the house, to the sprinkler, but I kept looking back to the right to see where you went. And that's when it happened. Your hand, the same hand that had waved to me a moment before, let go of this powder. It looked like a powder eyeshadow, brilliant and iridescent. It dispersed so gracefully over our house, flying across the small garden and in through the window of Mom and Dad's bedroom. This must have been on purpose, Inés. Even if I'd tried, I could not have done it with such precision.

I stopped moving. I was totally immobile. The water truck passed right in front of me. I heard the children yelling and laughing, but it seemed so far away, and you kept going, bicycling away with your front basket full of magazines. I could feel you smiling. I didn't see you smile, but I knew you were. Mission accomplished! This is the one that will break them apart! This is the one!

The sprinkler passed. Some children came back breathing heavily with their feet covered in mud. I just stood there. I had seen the magic happen. I wondered if I should I tell Mami. Was this important? Of course it was! But what to do?

Mami had been taking more pills from the head doctor recently to keep herself happy. If I told her, she would fixate and try to find another witch to counteract the spell. And this would mean I would have to travel with her to another city, to a scary house, and also, before that, that I would have to steal the money for this adventure from Dad, and I was scared of stealing from Dad, even though Mami always told me it was not stealing because she was going to use that money to keep us together so it was good.

But, on the other hand, if I said nothing and your *brujería* worked, Papi would leave us for you and you would not need me anymore and then who was going to let me get dolled up in drag?

Well, Grandma still would. But we only visited her every now and then, whereas with you I could do it anytime, as much and for as long as I wanted.

So I kept it to myself, Inés. I convinced myself I was doing it to keep stress away from Mami, but the truth is I was selfish. I hated that you wished her ill, but I still wanted to dress as a girl at your house.

I also hated that I didn't know what the actual spell was. I was afraid it wasn't just a love spell to get my father, that instead you might have made a death spell to have Mami die. After all, as I knew, you were not shy about killing mothers.

When you killed your mother, Inés . . .

. . . well, that's a strong way to put it.

If killing is only taking the life of someone, stabbing or suffocating or poisoning, then you didn't kill her. We can technically say that you didn't kill her, but then the question is: Is not stopping someone from dying murder too? I think maybe it is worse, although at the same time less criminal. And then, of course, you did it in front of an 8-year-old, not even thinking of the trauma you could be causing (yes, of course you caused me trauma, Inés, but hey, who didn't?)

Sometimes I wonder, what would I do if Doña Marchesi was having an allergic reaction to a peach she didn't know she was allergic to? Would I call the ambulance? Would I look for the EpiPen? I can visualize her dying, and judging me as she died, and at the same time begging me to save her. I can see her thought process: *This little whore survived all these years just to see me die. God help me! Kill me, but not in front of her!* And then I see me saving her, taking her to the same hospital where I was born, not because I want to but because someone is looking at me, like I was looking at you when you killed your mother, and this someone will tell stories of my bravery, of how I saved the doula of the town and how so many future children will owe their lives to my quick actions. I guess I love publicity!

Inés, we were comfortable with each other. It was the fucking '70s in Galvez; locks on doors were not a thing. I went in and out of your home as I pleased, put on your clothes and your long earrings and sat with you in front of your mom while she looked at me with no expression, unable to talk. We were comfortable with each other. We were aware of each other's secrets and knew what we both needed and what it cost, both to our wellbeing and our consciences.

Well, that's not quite true. We didn't know *all* each other's secrets. I always wondered what you would have done if you had known Miguel was giving me the adult treatment. I want to think you'd have helped, done something good, put a death spell on him. Would you have told Papi? Would you have been the heroine who brought this terribleness to light?

But then the question is, Inés: Would Papi have done something about it? Would he have found a way to activate some kind of goodness within himself? I think both you and I know that he wouldn't have been that person. I think you know this about Tito, this guy who loved you in secret, who had been putting his marriage at risk just to fuck you twice a week, three if it was a holiday: I think you know that he did not have what it took to protect his child.

The weird part is that you still loved him. Knowing he had no balls. No ambition in life to be anything. Not a good guy and not a bad guy. I guess, since people prefer someone who is not bad to someone who is bad, everyone thought he was good just because he wasn't terrible. I don't want you to think my opinion of you is so low that I think you too would have done nothing. But in reality, I can't think of anything good that you might have actually done.

But you didn't know. I had that secret from you when I was sitting there, in drag, with you and your paralyzed mother. It was nice to have your mother around. As a witness. Someone to share the girl I was with, someone who wasn't you or my grandma. Grandma encouraged me to wear drag because she loved me. You encouraged me because you loved my father and wanted me on your side, or at least not on my mother's side. But your mother, she had no incentive to let me do this. She just did. Of course, she was paralyzed, so she couldn't do anything to stop me from doing it, either. But it was some kind of limited assisted empowerment.

I loved going to your house. It was so clean, so perfectly ordered. Which was also terrifying, because if I did anything or touched anything or wore anything in your absence you would know. I would try to put things back precisely, but if anything was a centimeter off center (a cup facing the other way, a sneaker print by the closet, the smell of a sweaty child by the jewelry box), you'd notice. Such a thrilling feeling. I did things in secret and waited for you to uncover them and look at me and let me know it was ok.

Sometimes you would catch me in the act, but I knew what I could get away with. Like stealing a flower from a nice lady's garden. I loved you catching me. The familiar feeling, like a hand pressing my chest so hard I couldn't breathe, when you looked at me looking at my reflection in the bathroom mirror wearing my favorite (also your favorite) pearls. The relief of knowing you had to allow it. As long as I didn't say anything about you and Papi.

When I was there, it was as if I was part of the house, and only we knew.

So, Inés, that day. I came in like usual, and I saw you mashing sweet potatoes. I loved mashed sweet potatoes! I thought maybe you'd give me some if I waited. You did not look at me, but I sensed you felt my trouble and didn't even direct your eyes to it. You just kept mashing.

I sat on the mirror-like floor in the gallery connected to your huge kitchen. Lots of green colors in that kitchen. I started playing with the plastic flowers you had in a slightly green glass bottle. It was not a flower vase, it was a bottle, and when I took them out it was hard to put them back in it.

You dipped your middle finger in the pot and tried the potatoes. You took a very intentional breath, which made me believe they were just perfect. Perfect mashed sweet potatoes.

But you still didn't look at me. Instead, you walked over to your mom in her wheelchair. You moved her over, to accommodate your chair, and sat down in front of her, facing her. I never saw you being nasty to your mom. I never saw you being nice either.

You put a spoon of sweet potatoes in her mouth, and helped her lift her chin up so she would swallow, and then you did it again, but when you did it for the second time the amount in the spoon was bigger, much bigger. You placed it in her mouth gently, forced her chin up as you did before, and the sweet potatoes got stuck. Your mother choked, tears came out of her blue eyes, and she turned them to me, and you sat there, immobile, and I did too. We both saw this. You saw it in front of you and I saw you see it and we both did nothing.

We sat there, looking at her leaving.

And then you turned your neck and faced me. You needed me on your side. You needed me not to complain. To be ok with it when the time would come. Your eyes locked into my eyes, and all this energy travelled through my body holding plastic flowers in my hands.

Were you crying? I don't think so. You looked at me with care and love. Your eyes were full of love to her and to me and to yourself. It was terrifying, but I was not scared of you. There was a huge feeling of relief in the room. No more crushing food or mashing potatoes, no more coming back several times during the day to give her meds, no more washing her body or changing her dirty undies, no more giving her an extra sleeping pill on the days my father visited you.

I realized that that was the process of life and death. One moment you are alive, and then *puff*, you are not, and sometimes, as with this event, someone else could be responsible for it. Someone as close as a family member. Those things happen and that . . .

. . . I was going to say, "that is ok," but is it? Sometimes freedom takes radical actions to be achieved. And this one was yours.

Should I do this to Mami? I thought. All those times when she got in the way of my happiness. All those times I wished she would disappear. All that shame, hers about me and mine about her . . . gone.

༄

I had to take a couple of days away from this letter, Inés. Evaluating how I grew up required a couple of days. Also, as I mentioned, I am moving in with my boyfriend, and it is so complicated, you know?

Well, I guess you don't. You never moved. Anywhere or with anyone. Most importantly, not with my father, which I know was your dream. I have a hard time understanding this dream. Maybe we knew two different guys. Maybe Papi was a good lover and a terrible father? Like my mom: a great woman but a fucked-up mother. I just do not understand why you and her both were so obsessed with that prize, Ferdinando "Tito" Gentili. But you never moved in with him. You stayed all your life in the house where you were born.

I think after your mother's passing, you were confident the house would be yours. That beautiful, long house, full of windows. The entrance, simple: a metal door with textured glass that let you see when someone or something was on the other side, but not exactly who or what. Then that long gallery with those windows with a system where when you pulled down a handle they would open horizontally, but only part way. Louvred, I think they are called. Somehow the same concept as the door. See a bit, but not the whole thing.

On the other side of the gallery, three rooms with no windows, just doors—both onto the gallery and between the rooms. At the end of the gallery a huge bathroom, with a mirror, where I cross-dressed, and the kitchen and that little foyer where I sat and watched you get rid of your mother. Right next to the kitchen, the back door I snuck in through. And the whole thing, like I say, *impeccable*! What a treat to see yourself on the cheap reflective squares of the wood floors!

With your mother out of the picture, it must have seemed the universe was going to unveil itself to you. A chance to do you. To live your life without always coming home to take care of her, without taking her to the doctor, without any of those things you had to do just because you were the girl. Your brother didn't have to do anything. He had a life and made children while you were an unpaid nurse.

But now, you must have thought, you would have this big house for yourself and maybe, just maybe, now Tito would seriously consider leaving Esmeralda and moving in with you. And a simple spoon of mashed sweet potatoes had bought you this future. All you had to do was sit there and watch it happen, as I had, in that luminous space no one could clearly see from outside. Just the blurred silhouettes, innocent figures unable to be accused.

They didn't give you that.

Being such a serpent as you are, my dear, how did you fail to anticipate that they would screw you again, as they had been doing your whole life? What made you think they would ever give you a chance to be free? Maybe it was some innocence in you.

It didn't even take weeks after the murder. I was at my aunt Maria's house, right next to yours. My father's sister and mother in one house, and his mistress right next door! Now that I think about it, the two houses were not only next to each other but also of the same design, and you were a lot like Maria too: both destined, as the youngest girls, to remain unmarried and take care of your mothers; both destined to have feelings about it.

Dad had erected a sort of shed in what used to be Maria's garden. At that time he had a butcher's shop in it, alongside the abandoned remains of the sparkling-water machinery from his previous "impossible to fail" business. Mami had come over to get some steaks for lunch, and my Nonna Emma had seen her, and so, as usual when they met, a hardcore interchange of terrible words had begun.

"There she comes, *La Negra*. Go back to your tribe and leave my son alone," Emma would say.

"Go back to fucking Italy, you cunt!" Mami would respond.

"My cunt!" Emma screamed. "My cunt still hurts at times after you kicked me so hard in it."

Mami would laugh and say: "My feet rejoice every time you feel that pain, bitch."

These exchanges were a kind of free entertainment for everyone present: me, the clients of the butcher's shop, and probably you next door, Inés. But there was also a terrible feeling of anticipation about them, that maybe this would be the day they would go at each other again. Sometimes Mami would push her bicycle to the side with a flick of her hips, like she was getting ready to walk over and continue with the cunt-kicking.

Mami was younger, bigger, and stronger, and Nonna Emma was not stupid, so when she sensed the beginnings of a hip movement, she would shut up.

But if the hip movement didn't come, they would keep on yelling until my dad came out with the steaks, when they would lapse into uncomfortable silence. Kind of like in some action movies when everything stops and only one character moves. That was Dad, walking over slowly with the package of T-bones. Everyone was immobile until finally Mami would grab the package, place it in the basket, put one hand on each handle, and maneuver her leg over the bicycle from the back like you do with a horse, like men do, like a fucking boss, all without taking her eyes off Emma, who, mute, could only stand and watch her archenemy, still vibrant, still winning.

63

Then Dad would go back into the shop, and Emma would start yelling again, but now uselessly, because Mami, triumphant, was already far enough away not to hear anything.

Normally that was the end of the entertainment. But that specific day, after the scheduled argument, they came: your brother, Oscar, and his wife, Alicia (Nonna Emma would also call Alicia *La Negra*; it was so confusing, you never knew who she was being racist about). They came with a big truck with all their belongings, and we all watched as your brother pulled down some big panels of wood and brought them inside your house. Yours for the last time, I am afraid.

They created a wall that cut the gallery off right where the first room ended. That room was now to be "your room," and the mutilated part of the gallery next to it would be your living area. This was your "apartment." They put in a small stove and a refrigerator and that was it. They took the rest. Two big bedrooms, the huge kitchen, the foyer, and the bathroom. From then on every time you had to shit you needed to walk around the property to get to the outhouse at the back. To wash yourself, they let you use a little detached room that had previously been used for laundry. You had to shower by throwing water over your body with a cup.

Everyone wins! That was the feeling. You didn't win, and you had to let it happen. You went from having that huge home to a room and a half and whatever dignity you could keep after such a violation. I am sure you cried. I never saw you, but I know you did. I thought you would give up. All your work going to shit. All for nothing. But you didn't. Your plans got reshaped, reignited. You still wanted my dad, and you were not going to stop trying, and that meant you still had a use for me. And I, of course, still had a use for you. That's what we did. Use each other.

∽

I'm sorry, Inés, I had to stop again. It's hard to go through everything I have to go through with you in just one letter. But I don't think there will be a second one. I am trying to move on with my life, and all you are at this point is garbage and I need to take you out, for me but also for you. I don't think you intended any of the things you did to have such a permanent effect on me. You just wanted a smooth transition from Mami to you. But that didn't happen. And now I have to say some things. I think we both do.

My words may sound hateful. Some are, don't get me wrong. But my feelings for you are convoluted. You gave me something I really needed at the time. You were not the only one. Miguel was the same. My grandma Nata was the same. The difference is that Grandma Nata gave without further objectives. She got nothing from it. It was so natural for her to help me be happy. You wanted me on your side when the time came. You needed to create that pain for my mother, or imagine creating it. Whereas Grandma—what she did for me, she enjoyed.

She didn't just enjoy seeing me laugh while twirling around, dressed up with scarves tied to my belt loops and her longest necklaces twisted around my head as diadems and that light-blue eye shadow she never wore splashed over my eyelids with my fingers, dancing to the intro music to her favorite TV show, *Grandes Valores del Tango*. She didn't just enjoy this as a secret, in private. She enjoyed being seen with me in public.

Let me tell you a story, Inés. In the last year of elementary school, when I was about twelve, there was a sort of graduation festival to finish the year. You had to form a group with your friends, and pick somewhere in the world, and do a presentation about it. Some people picked Germany and made strudel. Some people picked India and recreated an Indian dance. Of course, nobody wanted to work with me, so Grandma said, "Don't worry, you'll do it on your own. We'll pick a place for you. I know there is a place for you, and it is in the United States, and it's called New York. So we are gonna go to the library, and we are going to learn about New York."

My Grandma was very dark; she looked Indian. They always gave her a hard time at the library, told her she couldn't be there. She went anyway. She told me, "If they say something, you just don't say anything, but I want you to know the library is for everybody. They can't kick you out of there." So we went to the library, and we read about New York, and somehow we came across this Nina Hagen song that was a hit then called "New York," and Grandma decided I should perform it.

She said, "We need to get you some hair. I know that your Aunt Maria is going to the doctor next week. We'll find out what time, and we'll steal one of her wigs." I found out it was Wednesday, and Grandma told me to get there as early as possible. I didn't sleep on Tuesday, so I was ready to go at 6 in the morning.

I met my grandma at Maria's house, next to yours, Inés. We opened the doors (like you, she had no locks) and went into her room and opened her wardrobe, and there were all her wigs. I tried on a blonde one with waves on the ends, and Grandma said, "Oh my God, you look so perfect," and I said, "Oh, Grandma, this is what I wanna be," and she said, "I know."

So we took the wig. The next problem was clothes. Mami wasn't very into fashion. The only thing she had enough of that she wouldn't notice it missing were her sweatpants. So Grandma said, "Bring me a pair of your mom's sweatpants." I brought her some pink sweatpants, and she had me try them on. They came up to my nipples. So Grandma said, "I'm gonna sew a bra to the pants," and then she took the sides in, so it was very tight on my body, and made me a sort of catsuit. But it still looked like sweatpants and a bra. So she took her jewelry box out and started sewing earrings, symmetrically in pairs, one on each side. When I danced, they would move and jingle and catch the light.

The final problem was that the catsuit was very tight. Grandma said, "I can see your dick," and I asked, "Is that bad?" She said, "No, it's not bad at all, but people may have an issue."

So she got me to steal one of Mami's black satin sheets, and she made a sort of peplum or ruffle for around my hips, and also a cape. So I had my blonde wig, my pink catsuit, my black cape, and off I went to the elementary-school graduation festival to sing Nina Hagen's "New York."

When we went into the hall, the teacher asked my grandma, "What is your grandson going to be doing?" And my grandmother said, "It's going to be a New York show." And the teacher said, "Oh, Frank Sinatra?" And my grandmother said, "Something like that." And then I went up on stage and started singing and people freaked the fuck out. They were whispering, booing, asking each other, "What just happened?" And my grandmother was there at the side of the hall, clapping and shouting, "YES, YES, YOU GO, CHILD."

They almost didn't graduate me, Inés, but it was worth it. And my grandma loved it. Not just because I was happy, but because everyone was so upset. She loved hearing others' mental screams. Seeing their teeth grinding when they saw me. She liked watching people hate seeing me be happy. As if my happiness, our happiness, would become bigger if someone disliked it. Whereas you, you would have been ashamed. You helped me in the shadows, inside your house—until it was not just your house but also *their* house.

After they chopped your house in half and took most of it, it became hard to cross-dress in such a small space. Oscar or Alicia could ask, *Why is this child in your house? What is this child doing?* Their two daughters could half-see me through the semi-transparent louvred windows and tattle about it. It was a pain. But on the other hand, there was Alejandro. Ali. Their son. Such a hot little ball of testosterone developing into a man. Gifted soccer players are so masculine. Even as children.

To tell you the truth, it wasn't me that seduced him. We seduced each other. I was already getting fucked by Miguel, so having sex was normal for me. When it became clear that Ali wanted me so bad, I didn't complain.

I did dream about him letting everyone know that he was my boyfriend, though of course he was never going to do that. I thought somehow, someday, he would just let everyone go fuck themselves and say: *This is my fucking girl and I love her!* A hopeless dream, like yours about my father, Inés. So on that I cannot fault you, darling. I did the same. Both you and I wished for years our men would claim us with pride, and they didn't.

Did you see that? Did you see that we shared the same pain? You may not have known about Miguel, but like most of the adults around me at the time, I'm sure you were aware Ali was fucking me. Nobody said anything. Did you all see me as Miguel saw me? As an adult woman? My sex with Ali was something I chose, something I wanted, something that I enjoyed so much, but still, we were children.

My aunt Maria definitely knew. One time Ali and I were fucking in one of her unused rooms, rooms like the ones you had in your house before they were taken. He was kneeling over me with his shorts down and Maria came in. She paused for about 30 seconds, then closed the door and never, ever mentioned it to me or anyone else. You, too, Inés, would see us sneaking out to the back of the patio of either your house or Maria's next door. You would see us coming back sweaty and breathing hard and smiling.

So many adults around me as a child did things that I'm not sure if I should be thanking them for or questioning. At the time, I thought it was great that you and Maria and my aunt Anita and the rest who knew about me and Ali didn't say anything. But now I think, why did you all see that as normal? And if you knew about that, did you also know about Miguel getting his fat body over mine, a child, and forcing himself into my little body? Was that also normal?

But I left Galvez, of course. I still heard stories about you. Anita told me once that you became bitter after doing the vinegar diet. She told me you fucked your body, your mind, and everything else with the vinegar diet, drinking excessive amounts of vinegar instead of eating. That was it, just vinegar, that was the diet. Simple and effective. You shrunk in size in a matter of weeks and had to be taken to the hospital. We didn't know about eating disorders at the time, or about mental health issues either. Mami would refer to her pills, which I know now were antidepressants, as *the ones that make me feel happy*.

I guess you both caused each other pain, even without kicks in the cunts. You wanted to be skinny as Mami could never be again. She wanted to be as happy as you seemed having my dad a couple of days a week, a couple of hours at a time.

I wonder why she didn't let him go. Of course, he never asked to go, the coward, but I am sure if he had, she would not have allowed it. How did you just put up with so little? One more time, Inés: Why keep being with someone who doesn't even have the balls to make you his woman?

Mami called me when you died. She called specifically to tell me. I wouldn't say she was delighted, but she did sound victorious. Accomplished. You were dead, Dad was too, and she survived you both. She was proud that you never achieved your goal. I wasn't sad to hear you were dead, either, but I also certainly wasn't happy. Because we shared the same experiences with men, I could sympathize with your failure, as I couldn't with whatever triumph Mami was experiencing.

I mean, I saw her point. For once, she won. For once she was not the sad woman, being cheated on, losing the battle. She was still there, and you and my dad had both died without getting to experience a relationship together, in public. Now you would never hold hands with him in the streets or say, "This is my husband." Never decide how to pay the mortgage as a team. But such a generous woman being happy about your misery was still hard for me to understand.

᠊ᡃ

I am finishing off this letter while flying back from Hawaii, Inés. My boyfriend and I went there for a week. I think I mentioned already that we are moving in together. Not to rub it in your face, but I can give myself a bit of a boost, right?

I thought so much about you during this process. I thought how much you dreamt of it. Moving in together. Very overrated, let me tell you. If I knew in advance what it would be like, I may not have done it. And my boyfriend's ex (did I mention this too?) is very upset about it. Not because she lost him (I'm not sure she cares about that), but because he left her for *me*. A trans woman. Now, a cis woman who gets in her feelings because her man leaves her for a trans woman—that is a new phenomenon in some ways. Groundbreaking. But this whole situation also smells so much like you.

On the one hand, it feels like a reaffirmation of Mami's desires completed through me. Victorious! I got me a man! Three generations of women in my family have now done what you could not do! On the other hand, I am taking him away from a woman who doesn't want him, but also doesn't want me to have him. Which is what you tried to do with my dad. So I am carrying out your desires, too. Would you be happy for me, vicariously, or would you be jealous and malevolent? I don't know. More importantly, the thing I have to tell you, Inés, which I just realized, is that I don't care either, not anymore.

You have followed me around, in my mind, my whole life, shown up in so many situations that reminded me of you. It always made me feel bad. But I won't feel that way anymore, Inés. You are not a paradigm of womanhood for me any longer, because now I understand you. I don't agree with all the shit that you did, but I get it. Some women, like you, like my mother, like me, just have to do what they have to do, to try to get what they need. The thing is, you never did get what you needed. With all your malice and witchery, you had such a sad life: so disappointed, so unachieved, without any kind of success. I'm glad it's not mine.

Cecilia

Alemana

Alemana,

I am so upset at myself because I don't even remember your name. Was it Claudia? Marissa? I guess in the whole *relevant name* category of my memory, yours didn't make it.

What we called you had more relevance for me than your real name. *Alemana*. "The German." Even now, it evokes a sense of envy of all the things I was not. Lacking those things put me (still puts me) on the lower end of the scale. You had them all, and, I understood, that meant your life was better. Let me itemize:

Incredible blue eyes, like a crystal, an extraordinarily faceted set of bright sapphires that with each little change of angle displayed to us different colors of sky. And, as if that were not enough, your eyes were also shaped like almonds, and your eyelashes, a touch darker than your blond hair, framed and highlighted them. The ultimate slap in the face to anyone looking.

Short blond hair, cut like Lady Diana's, with natural highlights; hair that would somehow arrange itself perfectly whenever you got up in the morning, apparently without even the need for a comb.

The perfect athletic body, but in the form of a little girl. Like a miniature of the models in the magazines that every striving lower-middle-class woman in our town who had (thanks to a strategic pregnancy) managed to land an accountant or public notary devoured in her quest for continued beauty relevance.

(Though all this, Alemana, on the closest inspection, was somewhat undercut by your feet and hands. They were the feet and hands of an old lady. They were strange to me at first, but later, when I understood the context of your life, they made sense.)

You were like a storm. One morning, out of nowhere, we all woke up to this Aryan invasion. The day before, your house had been just an old empty house over on the kind-of-busy street of the neighborhood. Then, at some point during the night, without anybody noticing, you appeared. A whole family of you, suddenly present, out of nowhere. Rude!

Of course, there were words spoken. Whispers. A semi-secret private meeting was convened in Miguel's wife's grocery store. So many of us packed ourselves in that the temperature rose to the point you could hear a steady pitter-patter of sweat drops hitting the floor. We were in extreme agony, but we were all too fascinated by your family to leave.

Nobody, it turned out, knew who the actual owner of that house was. Someone said that the set of houses to which yours belonged, over on the kind-of-busy street, had been constructed way before the rest of the neighborhood. They had been built, apparently, as a sort of *proof-of-concept* for a neighborhood of public housing, a prototype that had made all of our houses possible. But as life in public housing, especially at an experimental stage, was not for everyone, some people had quickly left. By the time the rest of the neighborhood had been built, the house you and your family had appeared in was already empty.

As a result, the gathering concluded, it was sadly impossible to conduct a proper inquiry into your origins and legitimacy: We didn't know whom to ask. As if it was our obligation, on which we were defaulting, to confirm that you were legally entitled to your residence, Alemana!

Instead, what we were left with was doubt. So much doubt. And curiosity. Delia Marchesi, the midwife and queen gossip of the town, was overwhelmed by curiosity and doubt to the point that the impossible happened: she couldn't form an opinion! It was killing her, but it didn't stop her. Together with the entourage of sycophants that always assisted with her agenda, she put forward a list of questions:

> Where did they come from?
> How many of them live there?
> Why are they there?
> Are they staying?
> Are they renting?
> Are they *squatting*?
> What does he do for a living?
> And most importantly . . .
> *Where is the mother?*

(My own mother, Alemana, in her usual way, kept herself out of this discussion. She was too aware of her own shortcomings to criticize others. However, I am certain that, if she had voiced her opinion, she would have agreed with those who thought that your father—after a short visual inspection of the area—had simply identified your house as a place to which he could bring you all and which you could just all occupy until something else came up, whereupon you could equally easily leave.)

ᔐ

I think perhaps it was actually because Delia Marchesi hated you so much that we became close. That is what happened a little later with my friendship with Juan Pablo, and it is also what happened with you. Against her will and without her knowledge, those she targeted with her dislikes and inquiries were brought together, as if by a magnetic force, and bound by her evil scrutiny. And so, a couple of days after the meeting in the grocery store, the inevitable happened: You and I found ourselves standing next to each other with nobody else around, and we started talking. It was clearly fated.

You could see me looking at you. I think you could see my thoughts, just as I was always able to see the thoughts of others. You saw my desire to be you, but you also saw that I wished for this without any malice towards your person. I wanted what you had for myself, but I didn't aspire to take it away. I wouldn't have tried to steal it, even if I could have. And of course, I couldn't have: What you had was not transferable, interchangeable, or open to theft. You were blond, and I was dark, and everything about me was brown, and I didn't like it, and there was nothing I could do about it. I knew this, and you also knew, I think, that I knew it.

I also think, however (and I hope), that you didn't see quite all my thoughts. I hope, back then, when we met, that you didn't realize I also thought it a waste, your beauty. I thought that although you had it, you didn't know what to do with it. I am ashamed to admit it, but that was my view at the time. You were so beautiful, but so unpolished. If you had been stuck with what I had, I thought, you would not have been as powerful as I was. But if I had what you had, I would be *so* powerful.

Looking at you, I learned again every time that I was not beautiful. This was hard, but not discouraging. It made me think that leveraging my personal capabilities was not just a possibility, it was a must. I could never be blond and my eyes would never turn blue and so this fucking complicated brain of mine was going to have to make up for it. But maybe I can admit something to you, Alemana: At that time, if I could have fusioned us into one person, I would have been happy to cease to exist as me. I would have been happy to be *us*. At the time.

You walked towards me. You were wearing a bikini. In fact, throughout that summer, that was all I ever saw you wearing. Nothing else. I looked at your callused, dirty, cracked feet. Approximately a month before, by my estimate, you had painted your nails a shiny pink. Now they were chipped. Not at all perfect, as I would have made them. You smiled and introduced yourself. You told me your name that I can't remember, but it was already public information that you were going to be called "Alemana." I believe your last name was also German.

The idea of treating you as my doll went through my mind. I told you I could get you a better color for your nail polish. By that point I was already very good at stealing beauty products. You told me no, you liked that pink. To me, this was confirmation that you had no sense of fashion. But then I thought, why make an effort with nail polish when the problem was the whole cracked and callused foot? Even the best color polish would not change the fact that you were constantly barefoot, and that you may not even have had shoes. I soon discarded the idea of treating you like a doll. You were too damn badly behaved.

Still, I recognized there was something that tied me to you, something I could not put my finger on. I knew you were there for a reason and that that reason was important. I knew I had to foster a relationship with you. Not a friendship, but a complicated relationship.

∽

I understood I could not be your accomplice or your sister. I also knew I had a terrible reputation already, and I really didn't need to further amplify the scandal that followed me around. It had become bad enough that even my mother had started paying attention and expressing concern. So it was clear that our relationship, whatever it was, would have to be under the radar.

I quickly figured out that the best way to be unnoticed was to keep in plain sight, but with a certain amount of moderation. We would not hang out too much, but when we did, we would definitely not act as if we were hiding something. And that is how it went down.

Within a short time, I came to know a significant amount about you. I could have given Delia Marchesi all the answers she wanted for her fact-finding campaign, if she'd asked. Of course she didn't ask—she hated me. But even if she had, Alemana, I wouldn't have told her anything. I would have kept quiet, or I would have lied to her face with conspiracy theories about your family to make her go even more crazy.

You had so many siblings it was difficult to keep track. All blond, all with blue eyes. It made me resentful that I hadn't inherited anything from my Italian father: Everything about me came from the indigenous side, through my mother. I remember thinking how easy everything would be for you, in life, whenever you decided to want it. Soon, though, I came to understand that you didn't want much for yourself, and that even if you had wanted anything, you had no time to want it in.

You weren't the oldest, but you were the oldest sister. There were a couple of boys born before you, and they looked like you, but somehow they were not handsome or sexy. It was as if your German genes could only benefit the female half of the family. I mean, you may disagree with me—I'm sure you have family pride—but I didn't find them attractive, and honestly, back then, there weren't many men I wasn't into. Maybe I found them unattractive because I was so focused on you, and on some level I was knew that if I had liked them too, that would have created friction? It was certainly strange. Even now, I still find most people I come across sexually attractive. But your brothers? No.

So there were your ugly older brothers, then you, and then three or four smaller ones. One was a baby who had just started walking. And your mother was gone. She had left your father for another man, a friend of the family. You told me you had caught them at it, that you had known it was going on, but that you didn't say anything. Despite your discretion, however, your mother had decided that dick was more important than her children, and she vanished.

I wondered (though I never asked) if your father was bad to your mother, or if it was just that she was overwhelmed by her attraction to this new man who had come into her life. I also wondered (and also never asked) if she had liked you, her children, at all. I wondered if you had feelings about the fact that she chose him over all of you. Like Delia Marchesi, I had many questions, but unlike her, I knew I should not ask them. Asking would just make you shut down. I knew I had to give you time, though I also could hardly wait to hear more.

I was so interested, Alemana, because this parental adultery was a point of connection between us. I wish we could have spoken openly and directly compared our experiences. I also knew my father was cheating on my mother, and I also was complicit in it, but somehow I knew Papi was never going to run away with Inés. Unlike your mother, he didn't have the balls. Whatever passion he had for Inés was too weak to make him risk leaving everything and going off somewhere to start a new life.

On the other hand, I also remembered thinking, many times, that my mother ought to leave and start somewhere new like yours had, that she secretly wanted this, that she would have loved it. Unfortunately, unlike your mother, she never had the good fortune to meet a man who was so handsome that he inspired her to begin an exodus and set out to find whatever it was she really wanted in life. If she had, I believe I would have been okay with that, with her being happy in another situation.

But, of course, I never found out. Mami stayed. Whereas your mother really did just leave. I wish I had talked with you properly about it. Not to comfort you, you understand. Caring for others is something I only learned how to do a couple of years ago. And at the time, we were children. For me, back then, everything was about me, and what I wanted was to learn from other people's experience. I knew I had to prepare for a hard life, and that the person I had to care for the most was myself, and maybe a small circle around me, and you were not part of that circle. Today, I wish I could have cared for you and given you some of whatever you needed. But you also came across as such a strong woman. You didn't give the impression that support was something necessary in your life.

It's funny, I just realized that I have always seen you as a woman and never as a girl. I guess I never saw myself as a child either, though. Because everyone else saw a boy, because I was not seen as a girl, I made myself a woman. And I recognized something like that in you, too. I don't know how you saw yourself, but I know you had all the responsibilities of a woman. As young as you were, you had to take on all the work of the house. You had to cook for everyone, wash clothes, care for your little siblings, and clean. When you told me this, then your callused feet and hard skin and burnt hands started to make sense.

Your father would leave in the morning, taking your older brothers with him to work on whatever assignment they had on the farms, and come back at night expecting dinner and a clean bed—although, you told me, he had never actually given you instructions to do all this. When your mom left there were no explanations, no discussions, no tears. There was just an unspoken, natural handing down of expectations. You just started doing all of it as if it was your duty. No questions, just an imperative to keep the house running and not show any emotions. On a motherless morning you simply became an eleven-year-old woman without any guidance. You simply did it. It happened just the way it happens to a queen.

That was how I explained it to myself at the time, anyway. I had learned about kings and queens and instantaneous succession from reading magazines. This idea that, when the old king or queen dies, the next one gets helplessly transformed into a queen straight away, without any gap, and immediately starts doing whatever queens are expected to do, like observing horse races and posing for Christmas-card photos. I translated your experience into this regal form, though your succession came without crowns, jewels, or pomp and circumstance. Perhaps I constructed this fantasy as a way of making what was happening to you seem bearable, because it was just devastating to witness.

And, of course, it was not only me who saw you as a woman. I am sure you noticed the way men looked at you, without seeing any innocence. You and I shared that experience, of not receiving respect or care, but instead being laid open to dirty thoughts. We were both disposable. For different reasons. I was a little faggot, and you were a little whore. This is why I am writing to you, Alemana. Because such different-looking girls sometimes have such similar experiences. And we did have at least one in common.

One day, I was hard at work trying to fit in with the children that hated me, looking around and wondering where you were. Susana Jimenez, my other friend at the time, was not there either, so I was even more obviously outside of whatever activity was entertaining everyone than usual. And then you came running around the corner into the park, shouting so hard. Your face was red and the capillaries in your eyes were saturated with blood and fountains of tears poured down your freckled cheeks. Everyone stopped. Then, right behind you, Miguel appeared, holding a small plastic bag full of vegetables, and I knew. I knew exactly what had happened.

I remember seeing the scene like it was a picture I was looking at, all the children in the foreground running towards you, and then you, and then behind you, away in the background, him. Paralyzed, terrified, angry. He looked at me as if I should do something to help him. I saw the fear in his eyes. This could be the end, he was thinking. But I could also see his frustration. *How could it be her who was doing this?* he was thinking. *What had gone wrong? How*, his eyes said, *did I make such a mistake? It shouldn't be her.* She shouldn't be the one who took him down. I could see his thoughts as if they were the subtitles of a movie in English I was watching in the cinema. *Not her. Not this little bitch. Not this insignificant whore.*

I, too, was paralyzed for a couple of seconds looking at him, reading his thoughts. And then I started walking slowly towards you. I could see that the group of children were starting to understand the words you were saying, and that some adults were even making their way to the scene.

"He trapped me behind the door, kissed me on the neck, and told me I was his as he put his hand in my bikini bottom and rubbed his fingers between my legs!" you said. Everyone turned their head to look at Miguel, who by now was also walking slowly towards you. I thought, *this is the time*. This is the time when I come through and tell them: This is what has been happening to me too. This is the time!

However, Miguel was an adult, and he had longer strides than me. Before I could get there, he had come up next to you, and he started yelling. He yelled that he was trying to help you with a bag of groceries. That he tried to hug you to show he cared for you, but you wouldn't let him. And then one of the adults, a woman, looked at you and told you he was just being nice and that you were mistaken.

My steps towards the group started to slow, and I understood. Nobody would believe you, nobody was going to take your side, you were going to be crucified. In the eyes of everyone, in the eyes of the whole neighborhood, the victim here was going to be him. The target of a damaged girl making up accusations in her head. So I stopped. I lost the moment, and as I lost it, I was relieved, and in my relief I turned around and walked away. At one point I think I turned to look back. In the distance I saw your blue eyes full of tears, looking at me as if you had expected more.

I don't think you knew (I suppose you still don't know) that Miguel had been having sex with me, that I had experienced his attentions too, that I could have corroborated your story. He had been, Alemana, and he kept on doing it for a long time. There is really no way you could have known this. But I think if you expected anyone to believe you it would have been me, and there I was, walking away. The thing is, it's like I already told you: Back then I had to look after myself first. Coming to your aid would have pushed me down a little, and I needed to keep my head above water. It was just not convenient for me to help you.

I don't believe we ever talked again. Not long after this event, your family disappeared in a single night, just as you had come into our lives. We all woke up to find that once-empty house empty again, as if you had never existed. You had vanished, gone to another small town to do it all over again.

〜

Before that, however—in fact, later that same day, the day you accused Miguel—I happened to walk by his house. He came out and whispered to me that he wanted to see me that night. That he was expecting me at 8 pm behind the hospital. That I was to meet him there as the day got dark.

I told Mami I wasn't going to music practice that night because of some reason or other, and, as always, she bought the lie. Then I showered (he liked me to be clean) and at a quarter to 8 I started walking over to the hospital, slowly, taking care not to sweat (he hated me to sweat). As I came around the hotel, I saw his Renault parked in the shadows. He opened the door and I got in, and he hugged me and kissed me on the lips. Then he took hold of my head by my neck, as if he was going to strangle me, and said, "Nobody could ever replace you, you are always going to be my little girl. There is nothing to worry about, my love." Then he told me he was going to make that night extra special and show me how much he loved me. I hid my little body in the front seat, slouched so no one would see me, and he drove off.

My first thought was that he was going to kill me, that I was going to be a murder victim, that this would be my fate. At least, I told myself, I would die like a girl. I found comfort in the idea. But he didn't kill me. Instead he took me to the Oasis Motel. It was my first time there (the first of many). I was of the opinion, at that time, that motels were very glamorous. I had actually asked Miguel, a few weeks before, what the Oasis looked like. He had replied that someday he would take me there. And now he was making good on his promise, giving me a "special night."

We parked. He told me to sit up and open the door and follow him up to the room. I can't even tell you, Alemana, how excited I was. Here I was, still in primary school, and I was being taken to the only motel in town! I would be the only one in school who even knew what it looked like! Admittedly, there was no one I could share this information with, but then I was used to not sharing anything. I had shared my feelings once, telling everyone I was a girl, and that had almost got me kicked out of school.

I entered the room. The whole room was a complete reflection of us, the facing wall covered in one huge mirror. He sat down on the bed, and I stood next to him, and he took hold of me from behind. His arms came around under my armpits, and he touched my non-existent breasts as if they existed, as if they were big enough to be squeezed, and then, as he always did, he murmured in my ear, "You are mine, you will always be mine, and if you are ever not then I will end life for the both of us." This was normal, but then he added something new. He whispered to me, "That little bitch tried to separate us by telling lies. She came to me, asking to be my girlfriend, and I told her I could only love you, and she lashed out at me and then went off running, yelling and screaming, you saw it! She hates us! But you know it now, you are the only one. Nobody can give me what you give me. No one can ever come between us. Only death."

He pressed his huge body against my back, hard, squeezing me until I was almost asphyxiated. I felt as if I was getting lost in his flesh. Then he let go and asked me to get naked, slowly. He explained that this time there was no need to rush. Nobody was going to come in unexpectedly, we were not in his car, there was no risk we would be found. For the first time, he told me, we could enjoy each other at our leisure. He pulled me into the bed and laid himself over my naked little body as if it was as big as his own.

I didn't believe him, of course, Alemana. I knew you were not lying. I knew he had tried to rape you like he did me. But I have to confess, it made me hate you. I hated you. He knew how to make me hate you. "Nobody can give me what you give me," he said, and I knew it was true. I was the only one who could give him what I did. But I also knew, and he knew I knew, that that was all I could give him. What you could have given him was different. I could not give him that, and somehow it made me jealous.

I hated that he wanted you, too. I hated that he would take the same risks to have you that he took to have me. I hated that there was anyone else he would do that for. And so when, shortly after, you disappeared, for a while I was happy. You were gone, with your whole family and your mass of blond hair and your stupid blue eyes, and I was still the only one. He was raping me and only me.

I wish I had found the courage to help you. It wasn't that I lacked courage—in many ways I was a very courageous girl. I had courage, but in that split second, I chose not to apply it. Maybe I was more like the others than I want to admit; maybe I also saw you as disposable. If I did, it was because I saw myself that way.

Even now, maybe I am being selfish. If you see this letter (I know it is unlikely), maybe you won't want to remember all this.

I hope you escaped like your mother did. I hope you are happy. I hope you are alive, as I am.

Best,

Cecilia

Helena

Hola Helena,

I wish so much I could have this conversation in person. I think I am finally at a point in my life where I could be totally honest with you, could just sit and speak without caring about how you felt about my words, without being scared that you might stop being my friend. I think now I would at last be able to show you everything. I think I would be able not only to take your friendship as a whole, with all your shit and flaws and beauty, but also finally to demand the same from you.

Such a shame that it took me so long.

But of course, we can't have a conversation in person. So instead I am writing you this letter. This feels a little unfair to you, since you cannot talk back, cannot tell me anything or refute any of my claims. It is also unfair that we cannot laugh together. But it is happening.

You are not the only one I am writing to. I have been writing to all the women who shaped my life as a child and young adult. I cannot explain to you how much my life makes sense when I go through all these memories, how much it all seems to be of a single piece. When I think of us talking, when I remember our friendship, I can see so clearly how you formed me. Things you said, ways we related: They still affect how I react to folks who need me, or how I think of myself when I see my image in the mirror. I have not seen you in so long, but you are still so present in all moments in my life. It is crazy. I don't know if I have to thank you or curse you. Because, as I am sure you always knew, it was not all good for me, my love.

Some shit is really bad, and as I said at the beginning, I am ready to tell you everything. And the fear that you might leave me, or that you might stop being my friend, is not a factor anymore.

So much of our friendship was always about this fear of mine. My mother, she couldn't stop being my mother because of who I was. I mean, she could try, and she did, often diminishing her role as a mother to a point that it was hardly even noticeable—but she was still my mother, and she still based much of her personal pride, her sense of purpose, her social being, on the fact she was a mother, even if it was unfortunate she had a child such as me. Eventually, through the years, she even found a way to be proud of me and show me the uncompromised kind of love that I am feeling for you right now.

But she only got there, I think, because she had no choice. All those years she and I were living in the same neighborhood, eating at the same table mostly every night, she couldn't go around saying, "This is not my child." Everyone knew I was her child. Even once I left, she couldn't avoid mentioning me as her daughter, because I was. It was a fact. A fact she could not get away from without being seen as a terrible person in the eyes of the whole of Galvez and its outlying towns.

But you had a choice: To deny me and avoid me, or to claim me as your friend and keep me. So that became a mission for me. To keep you keeping me. Knowing that it had to be okay for you to trash my name to your other friends and family, because it was important to your survival. Accepting that because your need to belong was imperative, you had to be free to take part in the general laughter at my expense at any time. And, also, knowing that there would be times when you would stick by my side. Keeping you keeping me was fundamental to my perception of my own value.

Ugh. Helena, I feel like with everyone I am writing to, I am sort of inventorying all the positive and negative things about our relationships. It is so incredible to me how we get paired in life. It's as if the universe knew that we needed each other and decided to give us a chance, then sat back to watch as we built a friendship while destroying each other at the same time. And I am learning to accept that there is no such thing as a good relationship, that you just have to decide how much shit, exactly, you are willing to put up with.

ى

You were so much older than me. Like ten years, maybe? But we had the same background. We had both come to live in the Fo.Na.Vi. government houses because it seemed like the better choice. (I am not sure what your worse-than-the-projects previous housing experience was. You never told me. There was always so much more immediate and pressing trouble.) And our mothers were so close. It was like they, too, were meant for each other. Maybe terrible husbands create these links.

Early every morning, your mother, Doña Presenta, would come over to our house, and the two of them would share a mate.

Often, Mami would give Presenta a cut of meat, which was pretty much our only currency. Then they would go about their days. Mami would go to work, ironing, cleaning. But after closing up the lyceum at 10 pm and riding her bike all the way back to the Fo.Na.Vi, she would go over to yours, where the two of them would watch TV and discharge on each other about everything that had gone wrong during the day. They were friends in misery. Your mother was the only person Mami could ever really be miserable with, with whom there was no need to pretend to be happy, or even nice.

Did they know each other before we suddenly became neighbors? I don't think they did, but as soon as they saw each other, they were immediately old friends—although for some reason, I believe, they went their separate ways in old age. Which leads me to wonder, Helena, if our friendship too would have ended completely, even if I hadn't left Galvez, even if we were still living in the same city—or, in your case, living.

I remember how gleeful our mothers both were that first day we all moved into the government housing. We now had a kitchen, a living room, two bedrooms and a bathroom. A mansion! That's how Mami presented it to me. They both saw opulence where you and I saw misery boxed with a bow. The first thing you ever said to me, when I met you that first day, was how, even in this supposedly better new place, you still had all the same shitty, stinky, broken furniture. You told me you didn't deserve to have to live this way.

At least you had furniture! We were basically living in an empty house, since all the furniture we had (ha! I just called it furniture. One crooked little table, a few chairs. We slept on the floor) could fit just in a small corner of the new place. But you wanted more. You said you knew there was a better life out there, and you were determined to find a way to it. At all costs. That pulled us together.

I too was certain there was a better life out there, but I never hated the one we had as intensely as you did. Maybe what you hated was less the limited improvement in your material circumstances, and more the fact that this supposed improvement was not going to change the reality of your family.

Your brother Ditto's mental disability was not going to be modified, the drooling from his lower lip wasn't going to stop, and the uncomfortable comments from others were not going to get any pleasanter. The people of Galvez were not going to be convinced that his incomprehensible words didn't mean harm, and they definitely were not going to stop judging him, or you, or your parents.

Your drunk, terrible father was still going to be there. Doña Presenta was still going to let him treat her like shit. He was going to continue drinking every night until he either attacked her or stumbled into bed or collapsed on the floor, unable to get up, lying there peeing himself and ranting while your mom cried and begged him to stop calling her names and dodged his drunken flailings. She was still going to ask you not to fight with him because she preferred peace over dignity and imposed that choice on you.

Your skin was not going to get any lighter. The creams for it were not going to work any better. Your hair was not going to become straight and your attempts at inducing Farrah Fawcett side-wings were never going to last any longer than 15 minutes.

And that new house in the projects would not give you what you were looking for. You were still going to feel ashamed of inviting anyone home and (like me) would have to continue coming up with evasions whenever someone asked where you lived.

All you really got from that move was me. But what a catch! A replacement little sibling who didn't have to take pills for seizures and who was able to articulate her thoughts and who adored you. A little someone to manipulate and pour all the hate inside you into and love intensely at the same time. I gave you a way to be on the other side of oppression. I would allow you to feel powerful. Exactly the kind of relationship I was already used to.

Me? I saw a friend, someone I could talk to, but most importantly, a living doll upon whom I could practice all the feminine arts which I was forbidden to use on myself. I could help dress you and style your hair; I could steal my Aunt Maria's shoes on the weekend so you could go to the club and have a different pair for once. It was a vicarious way to live my femininity. Inés allowed me to wear her clothes, but you, better yet, allowed me to dress you. My own dark-brown Barbie.

Enduring your attempts at psychological manipulation was not a concern for me. Despite my youth, I always felt I was a step ahead of you in those matters. Whenever you felt you had manipulated me into something, I was always aware of it. I told myself I was allowing you to manipulate me, and that this, in fact, was a way I was manipulating you. Maybe it was even true. Life had been a matter of exchange for me ever since I could remember. I was comfortable with tit-for-tat calculations: *I am giving you this because I am getting that*. It was second nature.

So what did I get? It wasn't just that I got to do your hair. I was getting your stories. I was getting a way to imagine how life would be when I grew up. The first time I went to that night club, Django, I already knew where everything was. I was able to flawlessly navigate the whole night without ever looking like an idiot. Though I had never been, I was already adept, a familiar, because I had participated imaginatively with such intensity in all your trips there. And I was getting real skills. I apply a sickening eyeliner because I practiced on your eyelids for years. Thank you, love!

Whenever we hung out, it was always at your house. And it was always at night. I'm not sure why: You didn't have a job most of the time. But Mami was happy I was there, since she was at work cleaning at night, so if not for you I would have been by myself—or with my dad, which was basically the same.

If Dad came home, the days he wasn't seeing Inés or one of his other ladies or hanging out at his butcher's shop having an *asado* with his friends, he would get home around 9 pm. To his credit, he cooked dinner: always the same one. A T-bone in the pan. If he was in a good mood he might throw in some onions and peppers, but he never made a side. Too much work.

What do you talk about with a dad who's a hardcore dude, who makes his living from butchering animals, and whose idea of a good time is an extramarital affair you're not meant to admit you know about? I was such an over-the-top butterfly! Not just a butterfly, but a butterfly sipping pollen from a delicate blushing rose that smelled like the nectar of the gods! That was me. Basically, we were total opposites.

Our only resemblance was our interest in sex (but such different kinds of interest, in such different kinds of sex!) and our noses. And as for my nose, I took care of that, three times over! When I look at my life nowadays, I kind of like people who are opposites to me. I find it interesting to chat or build relationships with them. But at the time it was impossible to build a relationship with my father. I think we both tried to make it feel and look like a normal encounter, but it was tense, fake, full of lies from both ends, and full of the understanding that the other was lying and that these lies were not to be contested. There was never violence, like with your father, or even shade. It was just nothing between us.

So the days Dad would show up, I would have dinner with him and then I would run to your house, but the many days he didn't come home I would be at yours early. If I was there early, your dad would still be mildly drunk—fun drunk—being nice and funny, touchy at times in not-the-most-appropriate ways, but somehow not disrespectful. It was the '70s. Prudishness was not the style, especially in men, and as for me, being the kind of child I was, being touched didn't seem like a big deal. At least he wasn't fucking me in the ass!

It was hard not to stare at your dad's nose. It was completely red. "That is what happens to drunks," you told me. "You can always tell someone is a drunk because of their nose." You were so disgusted by him. I remember wondering whether, if he hadn't been so drunk most of the time, you would have hated him less. Was your disgust really about the drinking, or was it about the violence or the poverty you were living in? Now I think it all seems inseparable. There was no way for him to make more money, because he couldn't work, because he drank too much, and since he couldn't work, it was necessary for him to drink too much as a way to use up his time—an entertainment always climaxing with a slap, usually at your mother.

"Why does she allow him to hit her like that?" you used to ask me. "She could hit him back, hard, deadly hard." As you pronounced the word *deadly*, with its implication of potential murder, you would always raise your right eyebrow, like the evil dame in a telenovela. I spent hours trying to learn how to do that!

Why did she let him? Why did you? He was often almost incapacitated, inebriated to the point where he had to be carried into the bedroom like a sack of flour. If she had defended herself, or if you had, if you had conspired together to kill him, if you had just happened one night to let him fall to the floor too hard so he hit his head and died, I would have understood and kept your secret. You wouldn't have been the only person in my life to have murdered a parent! But I knew that was not going to happen, ever. Your mother never even seemed to consider it. I think she thought, *This is my Calvary. I have to live with it and be thankful for my family*. So Argentinean of her!

Nobody could cook like your mother. Mami was a decent cook, but her thing was baking. Doña Presenta, on the other hand, would make the most delicious stews with basically no money. It was all, she said, in the movement of her hand as she was stirring . As if she was able to draw out taste with a flick of her wrist. She was always so focused when she cooked—the only thing she would allow to distract her was the necessity of checking on your dad's alcohol intake. She would keep an eye out for what happened when his glass was empty.

Was he still pouring his drinks himself? Then it was good! You would all be able to sit down and eat dinner without major incident. Had he started asking Ditto to pour it for him? Shit, that was trouble! She would catch Ditto's eye, and the message was simple: *Less, Ditto, less. Don't go all the way up.* But it was risky. If your dad noticed the exchange of glances, he would start to yell, "Up to the top, Ditto, I want it to overflow!" and laugh, and then give Presenta a hard look, conveying the message: *You don't fool me, bitch.*

Ditto, terrified of what might be about to go down, would dry the drool dripping from the left side of his mouth and try to make some comment about whatever was happening on the television, hoping your dad would take the bait and get distracted. Otherwise you would all have to listen to your dad belittling your mom for hours.

I can't remember your brother's actual name. *Ditto* came from *Armand . . . dito*? Oh, I wish I could remember!

You, like me, were lucky. We each had a room to ourselves. Me because my brother had left to live with the bourgeois part of the family, and you because you had persuaded the family your brother should sleep in the living room in a single bed, even though there were two beds in your room. Every night when I left your house, late, I would see him lying there with eyes wide open, waiting for us to stop making noise, because any noise came with the possibility of waking up your dad. Ditto's eyes said to me: *Begone! I want to sleep, and at every movement, in this house, shit can start again if he wakes up!*

～

As I write this letter, love, I am worried I am being unfair to you, that what I am going to say will make you look like the bad guy in the movie of my life. For this reason I have been try-ing to find nice things to say about you, good memories of our relationship, but I have to tell you, it is not easy. You did some terrible things, and what is more, they were usually things that not only harmed me, but harmed me in order to benefit you and better your wellbeing. I don't think you were fully aware that you were exploiting me in this way, and I don't exactly blame you for it. There are times in my life when I have exploited people too! Many of my desires or needs have seemed to me so pressing and imperative, I didn't stop to consider who was paying for them. So I don't blame you, but I don't excuse you, either. Somehow those two things live together.

When I told you about Miguel, I believe I was about 11 or 12. Several years of contemplation had led to this disclosure, though in the end I told you, not as a result of finally making a decision, but because I found myself with no choice. Grandma had gifted me a beautiful pair of white underwear, and one day, after seeing Miguel in his car, I noticed there was blood on them. I didn't know what to do. I tried to wash them, but the stain would not come out, and I knew Mami would see it. I couldn't destroy them or throw them out: they would be missed. *Where are those nice underwear Abu gave you?* What was I going to do? So I armed myself with courage, and that night, as I sat in the bed parallel to yours (where sometimes I would stay overnight), and as you sat in front of me in yours, I told you everything.

I think I was hoping for something specific, love: I was hoping you would do the right thing. I really expected you to jump over to me and hug my whole body with yours, and then, the next day, go over to my house and talk with my mother and tell her about the situation. I expected you to come up with a plan to make it right. I expected you to understand that it was in your power to give me what I needed from Miguel without making my behind bleed. You were uniquely positioned to do that. You knew about me, the real me. I showed you myself, and you allowed me to be your sister. Yes, you asked for things in return, but as I said, I took that as fair exchange. I thought you would be sick to your stomach, I thought you would cry compulsively, unable to grasp the idea that I had been going through such a nightmare, just to get a sort of affirmation that you could also give me, that anyone, for that matter, could give me. I thought your mind would be unable to reconcile itself to the idea that this famous singer and city hero was secretly such a monster. I thought you would hate him.

"It is time for you to think about how you are going to use this in your favor," you told me.

I recall being paralyzed. I minimally shook my head from side to side and felt my brain reverberate inside my skull, like it was getting smaller and was now able to hit the walls of bone and make an internal rattling noise.

"What favor?" I responded.

You came over and sat down on my bed. You shuffled your ass around, pushed your feet under it, raised your knees, and crossed your forearms over them. You were signaling that you were going to drop a gem. "You are not stupid," you said. "You very well know that what he is doing is bad and that he needs to keep it in the dark in order to continue doing it. Or what?" You raised your voice and suddenly smiled. "Do you think he's going to wait until you are older and leave his family for you?"

I felt my eyebrows contracting. I said, "No." Very low. I thought to myself, *What makes you think I would ever want that?*

"Well, that's right," you went on. "He's never going to leave them. Not just because you are a boy, and he won't leave his family for a boy, but also because you are a child and he could go to jail. And this gives you what?" You waited, but I didn't respond, so you asked again a bit louder. "WHAT?"

"I don't know . . . " I muttered.

You leaned closer to my face and pointed your index finger at me and then quickly flicked it to the side and tapped my temple. "It gives you POWER," you said. "Now pay attention, my darling, because you are going learn so much right now."

You explained to me that this could help us both, and you quickly came up with a plan. Which was that I would go to Miguel and tell him that I was having feelings about our relationship and that I thought I needed to tell Mami about it. If I did this, you said, one of two things would happen. Either he would either freak out and try to hit me, or he would start crying. You told me that this moment would be crucial. If he looked at all like he was moving towards violence I needed to tell him right away that I had already told someone about what he had been doing and that that someone was you. This, you said, would minimize the risk of him killing me on the spot.

I said, "Wait, he might kill me? Maybe I should just keep letting him fuck me. I want to be alive."

"Don't be stupid," you laughed, "he's not going to kill you once he knows I know. Once he knows that, he'll know I am responsible for keeping you alive, and trust me, my darling, I will protect our bond forever."

Weirdly, I did not feel any relief hearing this.

We proceeded to act out the conversation, as practice. You were Miguel and I was me and we went through all possible scenarios. Him getting violent, him begging me to go back to you and tell you it was a lie, him running out and leaving me alone, him crying . . .

All these scenarios, according to you, were supposed to lead to the same outcome. He would realize he had a responsibility to help me in return for what he took from me, but that what he had been giving me—affirmation of my gender—was something I didn't need from him any longer. You were now giving me all the acceptance of the fact I was a girl that I craved, so he was no longer necessary for this. As such, he had a choice to make. He could keep me, but only as long as I felt cared for in other ways. If he chose to do that, then in return, I would unconditionally remain by his side, giving him what he needed.

We also discussed how I could discourage him from imagining any way to care for and help me that was not money. That was very clear. "The end goal," you said, "is for him to give you money. Not only this time, but forever."

I said that this sounded like extortion. "No," you told me, "it is survival. This is what we need to do to get what we need to get. This is what," you went on (and I now realize this part of your narrative was very carefully calculated to appeal to me), "this is what we women have. This is what we can use to go through life. You and I have it. And it is sacred to learn that it has power."

I can see now that those words of yours made me feel included in the group of women with a fullness and decisiveness I had never felt before, because you were right: I did have that power. I see, looking back, how my whole life I have gone on to do this, to try to use sex in this way, as power, over and over again, just as you said a woman does.

"Don't be a fool," you told me. "Don't be like all those stupid girls who just give it out for free. This is the only thing you have, this is the only thing that you can use, and it depends on you, what you will get in return. Him, he needs it, and you, you have it. Basic theory of exchange."

You mentioned my brother, Claudio. You asked me to note how cleverly he had used the hate my father's mother bore against her daughter-in-law, my mother. He had been taken to live with Nonna Emma in her bourgeois house not because she loved him, but because he knew how to give her what she needed. Emma was gaining Mami's misery and Claudio was getting every material thing he wanted: A big house in a desirable neighborhood, clothes and sneakers, and most importantly, the freedom to do whatever he wanted—just as long as, in return, he stayed there, in her house, reminding Mami that she had lost.

I feel as if I have lived the life of an adult for a long time, since a young age. But if I have to put my finger on it, it was after this talk with you that I felt like I graduated to adulthood. After this talk, I was supposed to go out and tell this man, Miguel, that his happiness, his existence, and his reputation were now in my hands, that after what had happened, I now had the power, and that he could make a choice to pay me for it or lose everything.

And I went out and did just that. It was easier than I thought. It felt like a natural path for him to take. I think he had even already contemplated such a scenario. Or at least, that he had been aware this was a possible outcome, and as he could not bring himself to stop seeing me, touching my skin, kissing my lips, when it came to him, he accepted it meekly.

I came back that night with money in my pocket. I went round to your house, walked through the living room, past your mother, sitting watching a television show, and your father, stinking of wine, half-asleep in his chair. I took all the bills Miguel had given me in my hands, and closed them into the shape of an egg. The door to your room was open and as I crossed the threshold, I leant back and closed it with my whole body. You looked at me, and as I walked over to you I saw the light in your eyes.

I opened my hands and the bills fell to the floor and we screamed so hard that Doña Presenta came to the door and knocked. "Is everything okay?" she asked.

"Yes," you said, "we are just laughing." You hugged me and you kissed me and I felt sisterhood.

The day after, we went shopping. For you. I was 11 or 12—if I had bought myself anything, people would have asked where I got the money, so instead we spent it on you. We bought you a dress and the most beautiful high heels I had ever seen in my life. You promised you would let me try them on in your room. I was so grateful that we were spending the money I procured by risking my life on clothes for you and that you were generous enough to share them with me. And you, you were so excited! In a couple of days it would be Saturday, and you would be able to go to the club wearing a whole new outfit, head to toe! You said that with the money I got from Miguel the next week, you were thinking of getting highlights, and I realized I had to keep doing this on a weekly basis. But you were happy and so was I, so it didn't matter.

ى

I know, love, you always dreamt that one day you would find a guy who would fall in love with you so deeply, who would desire you as Miguel desired me, that you would be able to get what you needed from him. What you needed was not just money, but a ring. You needed someone to marry you and take you out of that alcohol-stinking house.

What you dreamed of was of no more saving your mother from a beating, no more having to pretend your brother hadn't said something horrible to one of your friends, no more having to walk for an hour to get to a bar. What you dreamed of was a way out. Just as I was, you were determined to use whatever power you had to pull yourself up out of the government housing. As for me, I'm sure you told yourself I was helping you do just that.

Needless to say, it never happened. You ended up with a baby inside you by this divorced guy living with his mother. You moved in with them, but it was just a move from the frying pan to the fire, or as Mami would have said, *from Guatemala to Guatepeor*. Still, I'm sure you somehow felt triumphant because you got a man. You didn't get married because you couldn't, since this was Catholic Argentina and he had been married before to another woman, but still, you called him husband. Every time

I used an alternative word for him, like boyfriend, or partner, or *concubino*, you would immediately correct me: "husband."

Soon after that, I stopped giving you money. I didn't think you deserved it any more. And then we stopped being as close. I don't know why, exactly. Perhaps because we didn't need so much from each other. Yes, you used me; yes, you got some things you thought you needed out of me, perhaps by unfair means; but I also got some things I needed out of you. And Helena, by the end—by the time we began to grow apart—I felt sorry for you. I never told you that, because it would have offended you so much, but I am telling you now. I am still sorry for you.

Best,

Cecilia

PS: I fucked him too. Your husband, I mean.

Juan
Pablo

Mi Querido Juan Pablo,

You are probably asking yourself why I am writing you a letter. After all, we just spoke last week on the phone. We don't communicate as much as I need, but it is always so cool to know that you are my oldest friend. Regardless of all the various shady episodes at various times, you are still that first person I ever felt at home with.

Mami told me, almost as soon as we moved to the Fo.Na.Vi government houses, "Do not hang out with the chubby one who lives in that house on the corner looking at nowhere. That is the last house in this town, and he should also be the last person you ever talk to."

At the very same time, your mom was telling you the same thing about me. So funny! Folks try so hard to avoid the inevitable. As if anything could have stopped us from becoming best friends.

I have been writing a bunch of letters recently. Mostly, I have been writing some of the people in Galvez I have unfinished business with. People I need to say some things to. But these letters are very serious, and my life has come to seem so gloomy and terrible. So then I thought of writing to you, and couldn't prevent myself digging into this pleasure, as if your name alone could bring some happiness. I have a hard time thinking of you without a smile on your face.

Trust me, *querido*, I know you were not always happy. But you always portray yourself that way, a trick I have now picked up from you.

That's the best way to handle people, isn't it, the best way to insert yourself into their circles? By being fun and funny. I wish I had understood this when we were kids. Back then, I was always the recalcitrant faggot, the I-can't-stand-that-bitch little pillowbiter. You, on the other hand, were the funny fat vivacious child. "He's so creative," people would say. "His imagination is incredible."

I guess finding each other saved us. I am sure finding you saved me.

Like everything good in my life, our friendship had the weirdest, most inauspicious beginning. For some reason we decided the right and best way for us two little faggots to interact was by fucking. Needless to say, we were wrong about that!

We had been trying, I think, to follow parental advice and stay away from each other. But then one day it couldn't be helped. You were standing next to the newly installed electricity poles, a big deal because they were the first in town made of cement instead of wood. People were very concerned and developed all kinds of theories about them. You weren't concerned, though; you were nonchalantly leaning your weight against one for support. Then you saw me. And I saw you see me, and I just walked over. Our first words were banal and forgettable, then you directed the conversation towards sex.

What were we, 11? -ish? I would prefer to think so. It would be really scary if we were any younger. By that age I was fairly experienced. But you were bigger than me (next to you

I felt wonderfully delicate!) and seemed to know more, even though you were younger. You already felt like you were older. And of course, you were so gay. You told me we should fuck, and I, of course, agreed.

What was notable about this discussion: You were the first person I had met of around my own age for whom fucking was also a natural initial topic of interest. I wondered if we had had the same experiences. "How does he know what fucking is?" I asked myself. "Why does he feel so comfortable offering to fornicate as if we were exchanging football cards?"

My curiosity was immeasurable. That's why I thought, "Yes, I should do this." It was out of curiosity.

I told you to meet in the eucalyptus forest. I knew every part of it intimately, since it was where Alejandro had been taking me to fuck me. Not to my surprise, you were familiar with it, too.

That Alejandro! Inés' nephew, the handsome football player. I remember the way that, when he wanted to fuck, he would catch my eyes and then move his eyebrows up and to the side while performing a quick minor tilting of the head in the direction of the forest. Then I would just go there and wait for him. After a while he would meet me, and we would begin to argue about kissing. He never wanted to kiss me; he said that would make him gay, and he was not gay; but I liked kissing. Miguel—now *he* would spend a long time kissing. That was the only part of our sexual encounters that ever stimulated me. Miguel told me it was the best way to show his love. So of course I thought Alejandro should do the same: love me. But he was resistant. Though not smart.

When you and I talked last week, *querido*, you said something I can't stop thinking about. You said, "We were smarter than all of them," and it's true, to a certain extent we were able to outsmart them all. But why, if we were so smart, did we also let some of them fuck us up so badly?

Alejandro is the perfect example. I let him fuck me, but who really fucked who? Who won? I ask these questions as if a winner was necessary. When it came to kissing, Alejandro lost. "You don't want to kiss, you don't get to fuck me," I told him. He always conceded. Thinking about it now, I can't believe what a hungry bottom I was. Nowadays my ass is mostly off-limits, but at the time that was the only way I knew to interact with men. Until I met you, and we tried to fuck. Then I had to figure out a different method.

When you met me in the forest it was like a duel of bottoms. You tried to be the man for a bit, but your heart wasn't in it. You asked me to suck your dick (the gall!) and I tried for a while, but then I glanced up and saw the look of disgust on your face. Clearly this was not right. We were both "the girl"! We were not the ones who got sucked. We were more like those baby birds we had seen in *National Geographic* magazines, mouths open, waiting for their mothers to feed them, except instead of food we were waiting for dick. We quickly realized we would have to be friends. No room for sex. We were too much the same.

∾

What did it mean for us, throughout our teenage years, to be "girls," to have that role in society? We were the feminine faggots the boys could go to to get sucked off after leaving their girlfriends who didn't put out. We were convenient cum dumpsters for the stupid who didn't know how to get pussy. Again and again, using and being used. Getting to see the discontent on their faces after they shot, so regretful and so relieved at the same time.

The same boys whose dicks we sucked were also the ones who would laugh along when their friends yelled terrible things at us in the street. Though they would stop laughing if we shot them a dirty look, scared we might yell back, "What are you laughing at? I sucked your dick last night!"

We never did yell that. It would have meant a beating, and we didn't need more of those. I've had beatings for no reason often enough not to go looking for more. Still, it felt good to know that we had that power, if we'd been desperate enough to use it. And it felt great to know that these laughing boys would come back begging for more in a couple of days, and that we could just say no. I think you were more conscious of that power, and made better use of it, than me. I kept falling in love with them, each in turn. Though only if I felt their kisses were real, that they were not solely an obligation carried out to get to the blow job or the final goal: ass!

But I am getting ahead of myself. While we walked back together from the eucalyptuses, I wondered: *How does Juan Pablo know how everything works?* I didn't ask you then, but soon after—when we had, to the extreme disappointment and shame of our respective parents, became inseparable—I did. I told you about what Miguel was doing to me. And you told me Miguel was doing the same thing to you.

This wasn't the first time I had found out Miguel was abusing someone else. There was also a "real girl" I knew of that Miguel had tried to rape. When I found out about her, I was jealous because I thought she had something I didn't, but with you I wasn't, because we were the same. It was the first time I ever had that feeling, that "someone else is the same." You made sense of so much in my life. I could be gay because you were. I was being abused, but so were you. You even disliked Delia Marchesi nearly as much as I did—though she was friends with your mom, so she was less malevolent towards you.

What would our lives have been like in that nest of vipers we called our neighborhood if we had not ended up on the same block? Every single one of them was so incredibly weird in such various and specific ways, and yet they all looked on us as the weird ones. Together, we were able to look back at them in the same way. I wish I could say "without judgement," but we did judge them. Like how we were both so scared and intrigued by *las viejas Catanio*.

These were two old women who were widely suspected of being witches, evil witches. They lived together on the edge of the new government housing in an adobo hut exactly like the one in the books about witches. Wild rumors circulated among the neighborhood children about how, if they caught us, they would sacrifice us to the devil to keep themselves alive for a couple of extra years. They were terrifying but unavoidable. Every time any of us kids wanted to go into town, we had to pass their hut, and they would come out and yell at us.

Looking back, I suppose they knew we called them witches, and they had decided to play up to it. "Nice day to roast one of these little ones," they would say loudly to each other when they knew we could hear. "Child of the devil," they would scream as we sprinted by, afraid that this would be the day they would follow and catch us. In terms of actually catching anyone, it was the skinny one who worried me. She seemed to be fit and full of energy. But my greatest terror was the fat one. She looked mean and strong, able to chop a child's body up so it would never be found.

Now I'm sure you remember, *querido*, that my mother used to have certain obsessions. I wish she could have been obsessed with caring for me, but no, she was obsessed with things like finding a recipe and making it over and over again for weeks as if it was the only dish she could eat. One year during strawberry season, she got obsessed with strawberries with cream. She could whip a mean whipped cream, and she would soak the strawberries in wine and sugar overnight and then serve them with the cream poured over. After eating that dessert repeatedly for a week, not only because it was delicious, but because Mami would get really offended if I refused, I got very, very sick with awful indigestion. Then my most delirious nightmare became a reality. Mami said: "I am taking you to the Catanio ladies to cure your indigestion."

I tried everything: I begged; I cried; I planted myself on the floor, weeping hysterically, with mucus pouring from my nose all over my lips; I screamed: "You want me dead! You want to get rid of me! Give me to someone that is going to keep me alive! Not to them. I don't want to die! Grandma will have me with her! Let's ask her first!"

Explanations were not Mami's talent. As always, she was stressed about something else, most likely money, and didn't have the patience to discuss my concerns. She just wanted me to get well. So she grabbed me by my arm and headed to the door. When I went limp, she pulled me along the floor. Eventually I had no choice but to stand up on my two little feet in my little ortho-pedic boots and run with her towards inevitable death. As we got near their hut, I could smell wood fire burning on their patio. I imagined my flesh boiling in their big pot while they laughed and planned a side dish. I resigned myself to my imminent end.

Mami opened the wooden gate held in place with wire, pushed me inside, and closed it behind her. Then she clapped, really loud, until the skinny one came out and said, "Ohhh Esmeralda! What happened now? What brings you here with this little one?"

My first thought was *why do they know Mami?* And then it made sense: Clearly Mami was getting their witchcraft to keep Papi with her, to stop him from leaving . . . and now she was going to hand me over as payment! But then, instead of offering me up, Mami told them I had terrible indigestion. I revised my theory. Clearly they were witches, but it seemed they didn't kill children after all. They just did what witches do: witching!

I went from being terrified to terribly curious. What can they do? What is the extent of their powers?

They brought me into the hut. The place was horrible; I knew if I made it out, you would cross-examine me about what it was like in there. I tried to itemize the contents, but I was having too many feelings. The hut reminded me of how Mami and I had lived before we had moved to the government housing. There were two small beds and possessions scattered everywhere. No proper floor, just packed dirt. And the smell! Was it herbs or rotten meat or body odor? It almost made me retch—though that also may have been all the strawberries and cream I had eaten.

The skinny one threw me face-down onto one of the beds, so I was lying on my painful stomach. Then she removed my little pullover and t-shirt in one movement. Mami knelt down by the side of the bed to comfort me. Then the fat one came over, started pinching big chunks of flesh on my back, hard, and pulling them up until something inside me made a snapping noise. Once the noise came from inside me, she would let go. As she did this, my stomach started to feel better. Magically, I began to feel rested. Then she stopped. Mami stood up, and as if seizing the opportunity, the big lady leant down, laying her heavy body on top of mine, and whispered in my ear, "I can make you a girl." Then she quickly got up and left. I just lay there, paralyzed by this information.

I am not sure if I told you at the time, *querido*, about this offer I had received. I don't think I trusted you enough yet. You would think that, having already shared the sensitive information we had about what Miguel was doing to us both, I would have had the blind confidence to tell you about her whisper, but I suspect I didn't. I think I just told you we shouldn't be afraid of them anymore. That they were not bad women, they just wanted to be left alone. From then on, every time we walked by and they screamed at us, we screamed back to show we were not scared. After a while they just stopped screaming.

But for a long time, I fantasized about going back and accepting her proposition. I dreamt of falling asleep in the Catanios' smelly bed to wake up the next day as a girl. What a dream! Of course, I had learned from Disney movies that nothing magical came for free or lasted for long. But even if it was only for one night, like Cinderella, even if I didn't get to casually leave a shoe to be found by the prince, to imagine the opportunity was beautiful.

∽

What the fat Catanio offered me, *querido*, wasn't exactly what you provided. But you did offer me something: if not a space to be a girl, then at least a space to be. Not many people back then would have offered something like that, not for free. And between us, we made it work! I guess that is the reason for this letter. I really need to tell you that I could not have made it without you. I can't stop thinking about the life of a queer child without a friend, because for me, I am sure such a life wouldn't have lasted for long. You made me feel normal (to a certain extent), and I envied your grace, the way you were able to navigate life smartly. You were even able to market yourself as likeable. I always wished I could pull off that thing you did where people liked you! In this respect, I have come a long way over the years, but I was certainly not likeable as a young person.

When we started theater classes, I envied how you were able to get roles where your severe fagginess was an asset, in which your sentimental, melancholic homosexuality was theatrically productive. I think that is what separated us. You had opportunities. And how you took advantage of them! Eventually you even won a Martin Fierro award. The Argentinian Oscars! *Best New Actor or Actress 2013*. I didn't even get nominated for an AVN.

What was it that separated our faggotry? Why was it that Rogelio Borra, one of the many homosexuals in the shadows of Galvez and the director and chief writer of the theater troupe we joined, used to write plays specifically for you to shine, but never allowed me anything more than a walk-on as a straight man? Rogelio was such a sad person! We would make fun of him together. An emaciated faggot who lived with his religious mother and wore corduroy pants and never, to my knowledge, got laid.

In addition to standards like *A Streetcar Named Desire*, the troupe would perform the romantic comedies Rogelio persisted in writing. In these, the heterosexual romantic leads were always actually less important than you, the fun guy who held everything together and also, for some reason, always had to dress up as a woman at some point. Meanwhile, I would be instructed to pass through the back of one or two scenes in order to deliver some kind of stage direction, like "everybody hurry up" or "they're coming," and even on my delivery of these, Rogelio would always give me extreme notes. I think Rogelio hated how blatant I was. You had a little more subtlety. You he approved of. I think the disparate way he treated us wasn't just, for him, about highlighting you and your talent: it was about shunning me.

Of course, it is also possible that maybe, just maybe, you were a good actor and I was not. But I like to think I was good too, or could have been. It was just that none of the possible roles made sense for me. I could not perform as a funny boy, and of course, they would never give me a shot as the heroine. That always went to Norma for her beauty or Daniela for her talent. I was never seen as "beautiful," and I could not be "talented"

FALTAS

when that involved something as hateful as playing a male role, so after so many humiliating events, I stopped going. I just stood back and watched you shine.

Even though we were the same, *querido*, we were also different. Being trans deprived me of any possibility of achievement as a child. Either that, or the fact that we were really poor. Mami did manage to send me for free to the music school where she worked as a cleaner. She thought I would become a star of the musical galaxy, but of course, that didn't work out either. Success remained an unattainable dream, but your friendship got me through.

Watching you succeed, I felt as if someday, success would come for me, too. You do have this power of making people feel great about themselves. I mean, when you choose to. Because you can also make people feel terrible! But this was a power you never used against me. You only ever made me feel better. You even made an effort to include me in your circles—not that it did much good. I could always read it in their faces: their moment of happiness when they saw you—*Here comes Juan Pablo!*—and then their disappointment when they saw I was there, too.

〜

I started going to high school before you, and so was first to face the question of which cohort I would end up in: the morning, afternoon, or night classes. There was an unwritten hierarchy to this. When you applied for a job and told the interviewer you had a high school diploma, they'd ask, "What time of day did you attend?"

The rich kids, the ones with influential parents, went in the morning. The poorer ones, whose parents cleaned the rich people's houses or worked in their businesses, went in the afternoon. The night was for the hoes, the sluts, the stoners, the kids with "behavioral issues" or criminal records, and the mature students.

I knew I wasn't going to get into the morning. Supposedly it was a lottery, but even if I had been allocated a seat in the morning, Mami would surely have sold it! I was resigned to being in the afternoon. You, however, manipulated your parents into sending you to night school. So smart! That was where everyone we actually wanted to know was; it placed you under the least scrutiny from teachers; and class finishing at 11 pm meant you could go out directly from school and not come home until you wanted. And there I was, like a sucker, stuck taking the afternoon classes with the other poor kids.

There was Mariana, whose dad was a drunk and hit her mom: not a novelty in my world. There was Martin, the cool boy of the uncool group. He claimed not to understand why he wasn't on the morning shift, since all his friends were, as if we didn't all know it was because, cool as he was, he still didn't have money. There was Norma, who we knew from theatre, who I secretly hated because she could sound smart. Maybe she really was smart, but it always seemed just like another role she was playing. Maybe that was my real problem with her: envy.

Through Norma I learned about menstruation. Her sister had terrible menstrual cycles. We would go to Norma's house to do homework and hear her sister screaming in pain. I thought someone was torturing her in her room. Norma was only too happy to enlighten me. "This only happens once a month," she began, and she explained all women experienced this bleeding. When I asked her where, she told me *from between their legs*.

Then she told me some women, like her sister, had a really hard time during their period and others, like herself, didn't. She insinuated that when a woman suffered, it had to do with some diabolical force within herself. Which meant, of course, that she, Norma, was pure and angelic.

Finally, she told me it started happening to girls at a certain age. I believe she was certain it was 12 years old. I sensed she was enjoying letting me know this would not be the case with me, since I was already 14 and blood was not coming out—not naturally, anyway, but only when Miguel would fuck me hard.

I was upset at this further confirmation that I was not a normal girl. At the same time, I thought: Thank God I am not, because I for sure am closer to the devilish side, and my period would be filled with pain!

And then there was Gabriela. I became friends with her and, even more so, with her mother, Mary. Mary was known for being a whore, and Gabriela was showing all the signs of joining in the family tradition. I was comfortable with them because, like me, they were always involved with some kind of shady business.

Whenever they needed money, Mary would send Gabriela to ask some man for it. I went with her a couple of times. The men were always very uncomfortable: having this girl come round to their jobs or houses was like a public announcement that they were fucking her mom. It was very effective. Within minutes, we would be riding our bikes back to the house with the money Mary wanted. But then, out of nowhere, Mary hit the jackpot. One of the dudes she was fucking actually fell for her! Better yet, he was not only the rich owner of a marble company, he was also young and hot!

At this point, I already knew that men could be controlled by sex, but it was Mary who showed me this could become an art, a field of expertise. She showed me what it was possible to achieve with sex: This rich, handsome marble-business owner married her and built her a modern house with everything marble! And she had him build it right next to the little shitty one they had lived in before. It was a symbol, or a lesson: I made it from there, to here!

But I also learned from her that once you have a reputation, even if you get money, you don't always get respect. She enjoyed the dividends from everyone's kitchen counters, but they still thought she was a whore. They called her Crazy Mary. Not crazy as in *mental illness*, but as in *opens her legs too soon*. Mary's position was that she didn't need their respect. "I have their money," she would say, "and that's all I need."

For a long time I thought that was true, but as I look back, I think she also wanted to belong, to be a part of the city and feel accepted, and she didn't ever get that. I didn't, either. That is something I have always admired about you, *querido*. You found a way to be a part of that world, to be liked and even respected, without compromising who you were

∽

Mary also was part of something that changed me and changed my relationship with you. This was when I was 16. You would have been 14. As it happened, this one weekend, Mary and Gabriela had gone out of town, leaving Mary's new husband, Gaby's new dad, at home alone. And the thought occurred to me: *I wonder if I can make this handsome man want me?*

It was the first time I had really asked myself a question like that. Miguel had lied to me and manipulated me and forced himself into my body. Sex with Alejandro was desperate, a way of convincing myself that what Miguel did was normal. All the random assholes whose dicks we sucked were just a way of finding out we could be gay. But this was the first time, I think, I took the initiative of seducing someone I wanted. It was me doing it.

I went to their house, and as soon as he opened the door, I knew I wouldn't have to make him want me. I could see he wanted me already. He opened the door as if it was absolutely normal for me to have come round to see him, my friend's new father, and invited me in without saying a word. He just courteously swung his arm backwards, as if to indicate, "the house is yours, darling." He smiled at me as I removed my shoes.

When we started making love, he was not nervous like Miguel had been the first time. We didn't talk. He hugged me hard and gripped my body and then began to unbutton the jean shirt I was obsessed with and wore all the time. I pulled down my Adidas track pants by stepping on each leg with the other foot until they fell to the floor. And as they slid down, we did too, as if it had been choreographed. The entirety of my tan body was laid on the coldness of the marble. His body was heavy, but not like Miguel's: I wasn't asphyxiated by his weight. I could see my dark arms around his neck, against his much paler skin. I felt totally in control. The thought ran through my mind: "This is how this thing is enjoyable."

He moved off me, onto his side, and started kissing me. He began at the little hollow everyone in my family has at the base of our throats (Grandma used to say that was God's thumb-mark of approval, pressed into the clay when he felt he had made a good one). Then on down between my nipples to my belly button and then . . . further. *What the fuck is going on here?* I thought. None of the men I had had sex with (not even you, *querido*) had ever touched my dick. And from my point of view, it was just there by mistake. I mean, I knew that if I pulled it hard enough up and down I would get sexual relief. As it happened, I had done this many times, thinking of him. But I never imagined him touching it! And then he put it in his mouth.

What a predicament! Clearly this was not right. What was I supposed to do? And then I realized, *this feels wonderful*. The floor was cold and my balls were on fire. I pulled my head up and rested my upper body on my elbows and left my legs inert in a V. I wanted to see his green eyes under his raised blond eyebrows looking up, like he cared about how I was feeling. Such novelty!

Am I getting fucked after this? I wondered. The answer was no. He didn't fuck me as I expected, but it was not something I needed. He had done more: he had made me feel desirable. I mean, Miguel desired me, but it was forced. It didn't come naturally. Something was very wrong with it. Alejandro desired sex with me, but not *me*. He and all the rest of the other dudes, they just wanted to come. As soon as they ejaculated, I was discarded, like I didn't exist—until the next time.

This marble tycoon not only desired me and my anatomy, he actually gave a shit about my pleasure. It was the first time I felt cared for sexually. He had also shown me something I hadn't known: that my dick, even mine, could be used during sex. Contrary to what I thought, it had nothing to do with making me a man. He gave my body pleasure and, in the pleasure, it became mine. I realized that what I had I said to my grandma when I was small was in fact true: I was a girl with a peepee. This dude changed sex for me forever.

He never, *ever*, looked at me again. I wanted more, but it was clearly not my destiny for it to last. And it was not as if he tried to avoid me. He was even very pleasant when I came around to see Gaby—but no sex, not a hint. I didn't push matters, either. I am not sure why. Perhaps I had already got what I needed.

Maybe what I needed most of all was to tell you about it. Which of course I did straight away. You were jealous. Men liked me more than they liked you, and when I saw the look on your face as I told you about the marble tycoon, I realized this fact. Yes, people at large, the town, the other kids, the teachers and adults, liked you better. Yes, you were more "likeable" than I was. But the ones that mattered, the handsome men that we really wanted to be liked by, they liked me more. I started to see myself as better than you. I was magnanimous about it. Just as you invited me into your social circles, so I made sure to share the dick I so easily obtained.

This feeling of superiority was something I needed at that moment. I could try to fib here, pretend it was a natural feeling, something I couldn't resist. But the truth is I grasped onto it, this little feeling of superiority. Looking down at you put me in the first place at something. I feel terrible telling you this. It has been hard to come to understand myself as this person that I sometimes don't like at all.

What was also terrible, but what I don't feel bad about in the slightest, is that this encounter also taught me that I could have whatever other women had. I carried around with me for years the twisted pleasure of looking at other women, "real girls," and knowing, *bitch, I could have your man in a minute.* Even if it was just for a minute, even if nobody knew I had had him, even if was a dirty little secret between him and me—still, I could lay my hands on what they cherished the most. I could touch their little trophies whenever they looked away. Through the years I experienced this need many times. Only you and I know how many husbands I snatched!

5

It was around this time that we met Gustavo. What a shady bitch and what a joy of a person! I was the one who met him first, as part of my doomed attempts at a music career, and he immediately made it clear he didn't care for me. You would expect a fellow faggot to make you feel welcome, but he acted as if I wasn't there. It was only when he met you, and you intimated that you were friends with me, that he became willing to acknowledge my existence. The three of us then became a trio. Gustavo was something I didn't have words for then, but I have since found an English phrase that will do: he was "a walking read."

He was ruthless: nobody wanted to be the topic of his tongue! Subtly or bluntly, softly or loudly, pithily or extendedly, for hours, Gustavo could read another person for filth!

Be attentive, he taught us. *These straight women all hate us because we have something they don't. The children they proudly parade as the validation of their existence are also the reason they cannot go to the club every night, as we do. The ring they flash with arrogance is the symbol of their captivity in an almost certainly terrible marriage, a fetter attached to a chain that when evening comes will drag them back home to make dinner and perform other wifely duties.*

Whereas we, we can eat when we want, and we can also eat from their plates. Don't you think they suspect that their husbands sneak off to us for a quick blow job? Any time we want, we can either boldly announce this to them, or else merely suggest it. As they know perfectly well it is true, just a hint will suffice to bring them back to reality. So rejoice!

Gather dirt, he also taught us, *from everybody, because it's your best ammunition, and when they attack, or when they least expect it, you can drop it. If some straight woman dares to say something bitchy about what you're wearing, respond that this faggot nevertheless gets to choose what she wears, whereas she has to ask for her husband's approval of her ugly dress, and oh, trust me, mami, that dress is so ugly. Then hand her a copy of* Vogue *from your collection and wait for her to realize she doesn't have even the money to purchase the magazine, let alone the clothes it depicts, because she's drained as dry financially by domestic expenses and bills as her breasts are by milk pumps, expenses about which you don't have to worry.*

Somehow, although Gustavo had been living with his boyfriend Lalo for many years, nobody openly questioned it or gossiped. Or if someone did question it, everyone would quickly jump in to insist they were "friends," or that they "both loved art," as if loving art made you less of a faggot. I loved art. I could read music; I could analyze a whole sonata with my eyes closed. I spent four hours a day immersed in the arts at the Lyceum! People still saw me as the most belligerent fag.

I spent a lot of time trying to figure out this strange deference Gustavo received. Because, like me, he was not only queer as fuck, but also poor: how did he manage to get treated with respect? Were people just afraid of his sharp tongue? Or, maybe, was it that he was with someone who had a certain level of social prestige?

Lalo wasn't rich—he had a shitty job selling calculators—but he was from an old, well-known family, with the prestige of their name, and he also still held on to the grand family house on Avenida de Mayo. An actual castle! All of Lalo and Gustavo's money, which wasn't a lot, was sucked into this castle, but they must have thought it was worth it for the prestige it gave them. I realized the last recourse to succeed, if I couldn't get money, would be to get some kind of access to prestige—either of my own, or by being with someone who had it.

I remember thinking that if Mami died (her blood pressure was always through the roof because of the constant risk of being taken to court for money she owed), then people would have no reason to respect me at all, even a tiny bit, as they did now. There was no way I'd get a rich husband like Mary—no marble merchants for me—and there weren't many Lalos in Galvez who could be in a relationship with a homo with no shame and still command respect from everybody.

You and I were left with few choices: we either had to leave that fucking place or keep fighting forever, a never-ending fight that I didn't know if I could endure or even start. And even if I did keep fighting, what would that look like? I was afraid I would just become the new Tati Luna.

With the years, I have come to respect Tati Luna much more than I could ever have imagined. I wish I could see him and tell him. "Hi! You were so brave!" If I did, he would probably spit in my face and call me a ridiculous tranny. He would have the absolute right to do that. For us then, laughing at Tati was a way to not be the ones on the bottom. When everything was terrible, we would lift ourselves up by looking down on him.

Every time I start to think maybe I am a good person, the image of Tati, standing on that corner outside the bar where he was always to be found, underneath the green light of the pharmacy sign, picking up boys and being as much of a flaming faggot as he could possibly be—that image comes to haunt me.

I looked down on the one amongst us who was the most courageous, the only one that really didn't give a fuck about anybody. As I try to forgive myself for all the shit I did in the past, part of me wants to say, "That's what you had to do to survive!"

But I know we made a choice to feel as if we were better than him.

The three of us—you, Gustavo, and I—would sit inside that bar, looking out at Tati with his incredibly architectural hair designs, intended to conceal his baldness. Everything from the left side of his head was combed to the right, and everything from the right to the left, and somehow, through extreme teasing and the deployment of super-hold spray, the two together approximated the missing middle.

There is Tati wearing his helmet, we would say, *and today he is wearing eyeliner!* As if we too didn't secretly want to be wearing eyeliner. Somehow it was easy to make fun of him. But I could see him looking at me with the corner of his older eye and thinking, carry on little butterfly, you just keep trying to belong, I'll be out here being free.

I never had the courage to be as free as Tati Luna in Galvez. I, like you, only claimed for myself that kind of freedom when we went on nights out in Rosario. The Big City! We'd take the last bus in the evening, spend the whole night, and take the first bus back in the morning. During those times we experienced the ability to be whoever we wanted to be. But although you can be whoever you want in the big city, it comes with a cost: you're also nobody. This led us to a question: did we want to be free, or did we want to be somebody?

To begin with, we both chose freedom. We decided that we would leave Galvez. At any cost, we would find a way to become free nobodies. You, sooner than me, found a way to be both, to keep your freedom and become a somebody too. I feel like I'm just catching up.

But here I am talking about myself again. Clearly, *querido*, this letter I have written to you has turned out to be all about me. And it's about time! Things between you and me need to be about me more. This doesn't mean I love you any less: it means I love myself more. No one, I have learned, is going to write a starring role for me. The only way I will ever get to be the star of a play, as you did, is if I write it myself. I will be my own Rogelio Borra.

Cecilia

Abu

Abu,

How much I miss you I can't describe. I have been writing some letters to people from my childhood, and I have been describing some painful things, so I decided that to balance it out I had to turn to think about the utmost happiness I experienced as a child: You.

Of course you lived in the countryside, a significant drive away. But I saw you quite a lot, either when we came to you, or you came to us. The times we spent together in Galvez were great, although I don't think you always had a good time. Mami was a worry for you, consistently. Although it was not natural for you to judge, not her or anyone (especially not me), I am sure you disapproved of her choices in life. But the most amazing times were when I went to stay with you in San Martin. Then we had longer periods of time together, usually in the pleasant weather of spring or summer, and more importantly, Mami was not there.

Whenever I write about Mami it seems like my words carry the feeling that she was a bad person. Do I need to say that she wasn't? Though I am sure we can both agree that . . .

. . . I was going to say, "We can both agree that she was not a good mother," but I think it's closer to say she was just *not* a mother. She had the love and empathy of a good soul, but she was never motherly. I wonder where that absence came from?

I know that just because someone is a great grandma doesn't mean they were a great mother, but when I think of how unmotherly she was compared to how nurturing you were, there is a disconnect.

We are three generations of women: you, her, and then me. But there are so many similarities between you and me, whereas about Mami, everything is so foreign. As if she was not part of the chain.

And no, Abu, I am not questioning the legitimacy of your motherhood here. That you were the mother was always clear, despite all the confusion and strife around the question of who the fathers might be. Should we talk about this?

My understanding is that, at the very least, Aunt Elena's dad was not the man I called Grandpa. As a young child, Elena would take me (intentionally, specifically me) to visit "her family" all the time. It was hard to understand. She was your daughter, but not Grandpa's, but she called Grandpa "Daddy" and adored him, but also once a month we would go to see her other dad's family in another place. But just his family, not him. He wasn't there.

Where was he? I heard once that he was living in Brazil and had yet another family. I heard that he resented you and refused to even acknowledge Elena. Still, your husband, my grandpa, that angel called Angel, gave her his last name. And Aunt Elena loved him so much! But despite this, she also, for some reason, made herself go and visit her father's relatives. Why spend time with the family of a guy who is not there? A dad that left his daughter, not to mention, Abu, you as well? I get a feeling it was a way to remind them she existed. That she was made of her father, and that she could not be erased, even if he was absent.

Now, with TV and the Internet, it is more usual to see people in the same families with different parents, but at the time I had not been presented with such representations, and it felt very complicated. Although it did explain why Elena was black, because her other dad's family were much darker than us. It also caused me to have feelings about my own father. Elena's dad was physically absent, and my own father was technically physically present, but he always felt absent, and I remember thinking, what can I even say about Elena's dad's absence, when my own dad is so distant? Certainly her dad's absence didn't seem to hold Elena back at all. She knew she had to make a future for herself, and she did. She moved to Rosario and became a successful nurse.

Your second child was Lali, a good fat ball of uncle fun. Always laughing, always happy. He married and moved away to work on a farm with his wife. They had a hard time getting pregnant, but when they finally did, there was such a celebration! Then there was Mami, of course, and then your fourth, your favorite: Pichón, my Godfather and the nicest person I have ever met in my life.

Pichón was single. My other, wicked grandmother, my Nonna Emma, suggested this was because there was something wrong with him. In particular, she took great pleasure in telling me of the time he was rushed to the hospital from the barn where he was working after paramedics had to detach him from a cow milking machine, which he had stuck on his penis for the purpose of masturbation. When I heard this story from her,

I felt that your decision to select him as my Godfather was the right one, and that you must have somehow known we were destined to be a match! Pichón's sexuality was described by many people, many times, as "expansive." That, I believe, was why he was your favorite. As I was your favorite grandchild.

And then finally, Pety, the youngest. If Elena went to Rosario to become a nurse, Pety went to Rosario to become Pety. She got a nose job and became a model, but her final intention was always to marry a rich man, someone upper class. Eventually she married the failed son of a prominent politician.

A few years ago, Aunt Pety came to visit me in America. I asked her so many questions! One of the things I wanted to understand was why you seemed so drawn to the queer people in the family, like Pichón and me. Pety told me a story about a close friend you had years ago. This woman lived by herself on a small farm, but at some point she had a stroke and became very ill. She was unable to move from her bed. A doctor went to see her and determined she was not going to recover, and that someone would have to take care of her while she died. He suggested they could send a nurse or care worker, but you refused this offer, and she, with the few words she could muster, agreed. So you became the one taking care of her, washing her and feeding her by hand three times a day and changing her diapers until the end.

Aunt Pety said that you did this for about a month, and when the moment came, she went holding your hand. I asked her: "Do you think they were romantically involved, aunty?" She responded: "I thought they were." I almost cried. But that was not the real meat of the story. Petty told me that when this

woman died and her body was examined for the death certif-
icate, it was discovered that she had a vagina and also a small
penis. There was a huge fuss and turmoil in the village about
this discovery, and everyone was upset that you, who must have
known, because you had changed her diapers, had not disclosed
it to anyone. The doctor even confronted you, but you just walked
away, saying nothing. Pety also said you instructed your children
to do the same if anyone asked. Don't deny anything, but also
don't acknowledge anything—just fully ignore the question and
keep going. "We do not," Pety said you told them, "discuss anyone's private business without them present, and she definitely
is not coming back to take part in that discussion."

I loved you then, hearing this story, even more than I had
already loved you throughout my whole life. Everything made so
much sense. Everything! The liberties I possessed at your house
gave me an experience of the possibility of the life I needed, and
I, for once, had to give nothing in return, Grandma. Nothing at
all.

◡

Pety and I talked about so many things. Her visit was a
chance to clarify our history. She spent two months with me.
Slowly, as the time passed, we discussed even forbidden themes.
And one day she plainly stated: "I am sure you are aware of the
rumor about Grandpa not being my father, right?" I nodded yes
and she asked, "What do you think?" I told her that I couldn't
even remember how I found out, but that I had always known

and always understood that Grandma did what she had to in order to survive. Not only for her, but for the whole family.

The story goes that Pety's dad was not Grandpa Angel, but Mario Rizzi, the greengrocer. A much older man, known for being very rich while living very modestly. I can attest to that, at least, as I spent long hours playing at his house with all his vegetables. I loved going to deliver the produce with him on his wagon. I would help him pick out of his stock the part-rotten fruits and not-so-fresh vegetables that couldn't be sold, but from which he could rescue the good parts for his own dinner. He lectured me on how you could see a moldy apple as either half rotten or half healthy. "You should never throw an apple out," he would say, "until you have taken whatever is good in it, even if it is just a bite."

I wish I had managed to learn something about being frugal from him, Abu, but I didn't. I am still a mess when it comes to money, just like Mami, always struggling to resolve all the financial complications I get wrapped up in. I hate this. I hate to see so much of her in me. But you, of course, didn't have to worry so much about money, because Mario, as your last recourse, would always bail you out and "lend" you the money you needed. Like I say, you survived.

After I had picked through the produce, I would be allowed to help harness the horse to the front of the wagon. I remember the feel of the leather as we assembled the headstall, reins, and draft. Then he would push me up onto the carriage and clamber up after me. Over the years, as he aged, it gradually became more difficult for him to get into the seat. But once we were up there, it was magical. Slowly but steadily we would proceed from block to block. The carriage had a bell, and around the middle of each block we would ring it, and all the women would come out to get their produce and bargain for a better price. I think they all felt it was a matter of personal dignity to at least try to haggle, but they must all have known that he would never bend on his profit margin.

His one concession was that, for a few trusted people, he would allow credit. He had a logbook in which he would carefully write their debts, and every month, by the 5th or 6th, he would come to their doors to make sure those debts were paid. But it came with a cost: Fruits and vegetables had a higher price if you didn't pay cash. "If it goes to the book, it costs more," he would tell me. "It is like lending money; I have to get my share of it." The only one who didn't pay, Abu, and didn't get written in the book, was you, and nobody dared to ask why.

"Let the child take control of the horse," you would yell at him, and he would gently position me standing up between his open legs as he sat on the hard bench of the carriage, give me the reins, and gently whip the back of the horse so it would start galloping—and this incredible rush of excitement would come through my whole body! Oh, what beautiful memories, Grandma!

Pety confessed that she knew it was likely that she was Rizzi's daughter. She hinted that he'd helped her out with money when she moved to the big city and become a model after she got her nose job, for which he had also paid. She said none of this had ever seemed like an issue to her. She had love for Grandpa Angel as her father and for Mario as Mario, and she didn't care which of them she was genetically descended from. What was important was that she had been able to leave the village she grew up in and pursue her desires.

5

All your children, Abu, were able to do this. Mami moved to Galvez and pursued being married to my asshole father. Elena moved to Rosario and went to nursing school and pursued working and studying so hard she had almost no time to sleep. Lali pursued marrying and farming and having a family and being jolly. The only one who stayed close to you was Pichón, your favorite! He was always close to you until he died. He moved into your abandoned childhood home, a tiny building—hardly more than a hut—that he fixed up himself, somehow making it habitable, repairing the adobe walls with brick, installing a small kitchen, even bringing in actual electricity, although he had to fight the town council to get it. They didn't want to pay to bring power lines all the way out there just for him. But he made them. Stubborn as you, Abu!

You never went to that house, even after the remodeling. Not even after it had been made almost unrecognizable by Pichón's repairs. Eventually, you told me why. Of all the memories I have from your house, my memories of that narrative may be the most painful. You were born in that house, you told me. Your mother, my great-grandmother, was an indigenous woman, and your father was a white man, and, you said, he loved her and hated that he loved her. Also, he was a drunk. He would drink a huge amount and get so inebriated that the only thing that he could do was to let his anger out. Then your mother would have to stand between him and you children, taking the beatings herself while you all cried and begged him to stop. This would go on until he would finally black out. Then he would wake up with bloody hands and, apparently, no memory of what had happened, and the cycle would repeat.

Eventually one day, when he went to cash his paycheck in town and as usual spend most of it in a bar, your mother decided that she was not going to take it any longer. It was a cold winter night, and she started putting on all the warm clothes she could find and bundling up your younger sister, who was a baby, in a thick blanket. Trying to be helpful, you went to get coats for you and your younger brother. She stopped you and explained she couldn't take you with her. You told me you could clearly picture her, your mother, kneeling down in front of you and your brother, spelling it out.

"I can run," she said, "and I carry your baby sister, but you and your brother will slow us down Alejandrina. I know your father is going to come after me, and I need to get as far as I can as fast as possible. Plus, you have to be here so he won't notice absolute absence when he returns and go out and start looking for us tonight. If I can make it to the train station in an hour—it is no more than three or four kilometers—and catch the last train, then he can't follow me until tomorrow. You take care of your brother and I will take the baby. You will be fine."

You told me you cried so much, but without making noise. Just plain tears coming down ceaselessly as you watched them leave. Her boots crushed the grass outside the house, and you waited for her to look back, imagining that if she did, she would change her mind and take you too. She didn't look back.

When your father got home you helped him to bed, and when he woke up the day after, he did not say a word. He continued living the same life, as if your mother and the baby had never existed. After a while, some slightly less-poor relations took you in. You told me that when they came to take you, you cried and tried to refuse to go. You were still hoping she would come back to look for you in that house, and you were afraid she wouldn't find you. I recall crying when you told me, "I always wanted to touch my mother's braids, feel the feathers in the ends while she sang me songs of the Pachamama, mother of the land."

That is something else Pety and I talked about, but which you and I never discussed: you being indigenous. I don't think it was purposeful, or that you avoided it; we just didn't. Although I do remember that when I would work in your garden with you, that little piece of land Grandpa Angel had bought and fenced off for you, you would always say: "We paid for this land that was mine to begin with." After Pichón died, you started to put all your passion into that garden, growing the most beautiful flowers to bring to his tomb, where you would regularly spend whole mornings cleaning every centimeter of marble, hammering out every dent in all the plaques you made for him—one every year—reminding him how much you loved him.

When Pichón died, it was as if your life had broken up and you were just surviving, fighting the wish to go with him. I like to think I was able to serve as some kind of replacement for all that love. I am grateful you poured so much of it into me. He was the first dead person I ever saw in my life. I remember

Mami dressed me up in dark-blue corduroy pants and a white shirt and a brown sweater and sat in front of me on the bed in the new government house we had just moved into. She said, "Abu is very sad, and you know very well you are one of the most important sources of happiness in her life, so now, you have to find a way to take some of that gloominess away from her mind. You have to make her feel less sad. I am confident you can do it, and you know I never ask you for very much, but now I am asking this from you." I said yes, I would try really hard, and she hugged me and then we went to the wake.

When we got to your house, you were sitting next to the coffin, and I ran to you. You separated your hands from the rosary to open them to me, and as you covered me with your arms, I felt the soft texture of the shawl over your head rubbing my cheek. You said, "I lost my baby, I lost my Pichón." Then you asked me to kiss him. I was terrified, but Mami had asked me to make you happy, so when you placed your hands under my armpits and lifted me up towards the coffin, I didn't fight it. I saw his clasped hands holding each other, and then I saw his face. I craned my neck down towards his head and made my lips touch his cheek. I said, "Goodbye, Uncle Pichón." I felt as if I was in some kind of trance that only finished when my feet touched the ground again.

At the time, despite the rosary, you were attending the Baptist church. It was so convenient: it was just down the road. All the other churches required a long walk to get to. But nothing was the same after you lost him. In fact, I think it was a couple of weeks later, that day that you took me to the Sunday sermon. People were being submerged in a sunken pool constructed inside the church for the purpose of adult baptism. Soon after we arrived, one of the brothers pulled you aside and mentioned that I should not be wearing your earrings in church. You turned your head to him and told him that God wanted me to be happy, as it taught in the Bible, and that you were the conduit to that happiness, and your earrings were God's tool, so you were just letting God make me smile by allowing me to wear them. He quickly went away, then came back to request that we stay after the ceremony to talk with the pastor.

The pastor, it turned out, had a different account of the theological significance of the earrings. He said that it was the devil, and not God, who was asking that you let me wear your earrings, because God only asked for things that would bring no suffering. You raised your voice, which was unheard of in conversation with the pastor. You asked, "If God asks only things which bring no suffering, then why did he take my son and make me suffer as I am now?"

The pastor was taken back by your defiance. He said: "God takes the most beautiful flowers from his garden. We are all flowers, and Pichón was one of his favorites, and that is why he took him. He was never yours."

"Pastor," you replied, "all my flowers are mine, and I won't share them. Not even with God. I think your teachings and my Bible say different things. I want this child to be happy as God tells me we should be, and if you can't allow him to wear earrings during your sermon, then I can't bring him back, and as I can't bring him back, I can't come back either. God lives everywhere, and I will talk to him at home. I don't need to come here to do that. I will talk to God at home with my grandson next to me, wearing my earrings, as he wishes to. Do not come to my house. You and all your church members are not welcome. Goodbye."

That was the end of church, but not of your relationship with God. You continued to read the Bible to me every night until I fell asleep with most of your jewelry on.

〜

The distinction between you and Mami is so remarkable, Abu. How could she have been raised by you, and yet have no maternal instinct to show for it? Although Mami told me once you were not as wonderful to your own children as you were to me. Was this true? Perhaps it was. But even if you were only a fraction as good a mother as you were a grandmother, you would still have been doing better than she did. I cannot imagine you being so totally disengaged from your children as Mami was from me and Claudio. Just think about all those times I started school late because she didn't want to come get me from your house on time.

Claudio actually left when I was born and Mami just let that happen. I still can't understand it, Abu. How do you let your seven-year-old leave the house? Maybe Claudio would tell me if I could ask him. Sometimes I even imagine calling him up to do this. "Claudio, why did you leave? What happened?" But I can't call him. We are so distant that I don't even have a way to start that conversation. He is somehow a stranger to me. Whereas your children, as different as they were, were all so tight with one another. That could only come from having a mother who

held the family together. You may have been hard on them, but I
am sure at least you were something to them.

I know I sound as if I am judging Mami, and I have to
admit I am. I can't help it. When I put her motherhood next to
yours, it is hard to not make unflattering comparisons. And it
was not just my faggotry that you allowed and she hated. That is
part of it, but not all. You allowed it all, Abu! With you, everything I was was allowed.

You know, Abu, there are young folks here in America
who call me Mom, and at times I don't know what to do with
it. It almost makes me uncomfortable. I worked at a clinic for
many years and I helped them start hormones or change their
names or gender markers, things like that. I guess this support
was something they couldn't get from their family members,
and so when I gave it to them, we developed another kind of
relationship. They became my kids. But sometimes I can't deal
with them calling me Mom. I think I am worried that if I allow
someone to love me in that way, then I will find myself neglect-
ing them, and I will turn around and find I have become just like
Mami.

I want to tell myself that maybe your maternal instinct has
simply skipped a generation. Perhaps, just as I got your psoria-
sis, which Mami avoided, so I also got your motherhood. Maybe
that's so. Or maybe—even though I do resemble Mami in many
ways—despite this, because I am now older than she was when I
was a child, I am able to imitate the kind of mother she became
later in life, when she had a little more distance from me.

Abu, I swear, if I had known that what she needed to be
nice to me was distance, and that once I had left Galvez with the

truckload of trauma I had accumulated, I would nevertheless fairly quickly be able to establish a mother-daughter relationship with her for truly the first time, I would have done what Claudio did and left home when I was seven. Leave earlier, avoid the drama.

We didn't understand her. I think nobody did. Maybe one of those many times when Mami hinted she would prefer if I never came back from your house at the end of summer, I should have taken her up on it and stayed with you.

In the same way that your position out in the country offered me an immense space to run free and play, your kindness also offered me an immense space to be happy. What would it have been like to have gone and lived in that space? No Miguels, no Helenas, no Inéses, no Delia Marchesis, and only a limited amount of Mami, on weekends. Perhaps I would not have had all those years of pain. Perhaps I would have become who I am now thirty years earlier. Authentic for the first time.

All that pain made me strong, of course, but who wants to be strong? I wanted to be happy! And you wanted me to be happy, too. How remarkable to want another person to be happy. This is what I feel when I get one of these girls started on hormones. Who is ever happier than a transsexual starting on hormones? They all call me Mom, but maybe I should ask them to call me Grandma.

At times, when I am watching a movie and I loudly make a comment about what just happened as if someone was with me, even though I am alone, I see Mami all over me. But sometimes, when I tell my children I love them, I see you all over me, too.

When I think of you, I think of a woman who in her greatest pain was full of joy, and who understood that that joy was not to be kept.

I love you, Grandma.

Cecilia

Mami

Mami,

Some things never change. I am still lazy. Always waiting to the last minute to get things done, then rushing out something that is either brilliant or bullshit, in which case I will bullshit my way into making it look like it was brilliant. Just give me the space to talk, and I will bamboozle you into my favor.

But writing is different, Mami. Things stay on the paper. In writing, I can't recover from a mistake by sheer velocity: I have to go back and rewrite the whole thing. Writing this letter to you, I have had to go back and revise things so many times.

If you were alive, and this were truly a private letter, things would be simpler. You would not show it to anybody, right? No one else would ever read it, and I could say what I want without compunction. But you are not alive and the letter is public. Even so, I have not deleted anything. This letter is unredacted. I am going to say what I need to say, and I am not going to avoid offending you or hurting you. It has never been that way between us before! We have always offended and hurt each other without any guilt.

There, that's an example. As I write that, even though it is true, I hear voices of all the people who loved you come into my head, asking me, "How can you say something like that about Esme? How can you trash the memory of that saint who lived for you and suffered so much to raise you? How can you muddy the reputation of this amazing warrior who was the best friend I ever had?"

They loved you, and you loved them. Part of me wants to say I was jealous of that love, but really, I think I always knew that your tight friendships were actually a great way for me to have more freedom.

Whenever you were having mates with Adelina, it meant I had time to flirt with her son. He never actually paid attention to me, but at least I got to try! Whenever you spent a whole day baking one of your famous cakes for one of your friends, it meant I had time to hang out all day with Juan Pablo, planning our way out of Galvez.

It was an unspoken arrangement we had. You did you and I did me, and when you needed me, I was there. And when I needed you, you were there, too. When I needed you, it was mostly because I had got myself in trouble again. When you needed me, it was always because you needed money.

〜

These days I sometimes have a little money to spare. Your sister Pety came to visit me a couple of years ago, and before she left, she asked me to pay for her liposuction. It was cheap in Argentina, so I did. Then the surgery went wrong and she died. I feel so guilty. I thought I was doing something good for her, and then it ended like it did. But when Pety was visiting and still alive, we talked a lot about you and money. What, we wondered, did you do with money? What did you spend it on?

We couldn't figure it out. We considered gambling. I know you did like to play the numbers occasionally, but that could hardly have covered it. We considered a fancy man, but that was not your style. Eventually, all we could think of were presents, completely unnecessary expensive things, and *brujería*! Especially *brujería*. You loved your witches, and they loved your money. You were always in the market for a spell to help your luck or to help your friends. I remember you telling me, "I will travel to the North to see this witch who can help Gladys recover her husband. You have to stay with Grandma until I come back!"

You loved helping others and giving people what they wanted. I am not so different from you in that respect, Mami. Just look how I wanted to help Pety. I resemble you in so many ways that it is scary. I fought for a long time not to be like you, but at this point in my life, I am wondering if I should just give up and accept it. At least I will be remembered as a great friend! In any case, like you, I also am a mess with money. Based on myself, perhaps your problem was simply extreme disorganization, lots of bad decisions, and a terrible hopefulness and belief in magical solutions. Also like you, Mami, I don't have anyone to run to for help. Money is such a hard topic for people in the United States. But then, I guess you didn't have no-one—you had me. We had each other, and I have to say, we rarely failed us.

"Alejandro," you would say, "don't ask me why or for what or any kind of details, but I need money and you very well know the best way to get it." I did know. It was scary, but I accepted it needed to be done. You never laid out the consequences of not getting the money, but you always implied it would be bad for you. And I loved you so much and didn't want anything bad to happen to you. So I agreed to do it, every time. And every time, we made it work.

If Dad was working the morning shift at the butcher's shop, he would get up very early—around 6, or even earlier if he had to start from zero and dismember a whole cow. If it was one of those whole-cow days, that was the best, but any morning shift would do. While he was at work, we would practice the operation—a couple of times through at least.

Then, at 12:20 pm, Dad would come home for lunch, exhausted and hungry. Upon getting home, he would find you had made one of his favorite dishes. Winters were best of all because you could stew the shit out of some meat, add in a load of potatoes and carrots, and go heavy on the sauce so he would use a lot of bread sopping it all up. Once he had eaten this heavy meal, he would slowly move, almost catatonic, to the bedroom for his religiously-observed afternoon nap!

The operation would launch right away. You would casually go into the bedroom to get something and, instead of shutting the door on the way out, you would leave it ajar. Almost closed, but still open. Then we would stand in silence, as close to the door as we dared, to listen for the beginning of his snores. That would be the sign. He was out! Next, I would lie down on my stomach with a wool blanket between my body and the cold mosaics of the floor. Then I would start to crawl, fast but quietly, pulling the blanket with me for silence. The idea was to get it done in a breath. "We are experts," you would say.

Clawing my fingers on the floor, I would push my body across the room and under the bed, heading directly to Dad's pants. Sometimes it was hard to see them: he liked his room dark. If that was so, I would use his shoes as a guide—he always dropped the pants next to his shoes.

As I got closer, I would look back at you to make sure it was safe to proceed. You would just nod your head down without taking your eyes off him, as if saying, *continue*.

Now came the most difficult and nerve-racking part. Quickly, I would inspect the pockets and, with a simple touch, find out which one held the money. It was important to do this without hesitation. "Hesitation will make you make mistakes," you would say, "and mistakes are expensive."

Once I found the money, I would insert my hand into the pocket and remove the whole wad of bills, usually folded in half and secured with several thin rubber bands crossing in both directions, with the intention of creating a barrier that we could not penetrate. But we always did penetrate it. You had instructed me in the correct method.

During our morning practices, you would give me bundles of dozens of pieces of paper the exact size of bills. You cut them out from pages recovered from the garbage at work. It was an early form of recycling. You would truss them up with the same kind of rubber bands Dad used, then drill me as I tried to undo them: "Pull the band with both hands without unnecessary stretching, and once you are not touching the bundle any more, move it out and close your hands and let it fall on the floor. Then move to the second one, third one, and so forth. FAST! No time to worry about noises. If you are too afraid of making a noise, you will make it. If you are certain of what you are doing, it will be silent."

Daddy was smart. He must have known it was impossible to stop us, but he would still try to reduce our haul by mixing the bills so that in the dark I wouldn't know what I was taking. But you, Mami, were smarter. You taught me to feel them, to tell the difference between a twenty and a hundred just with my fingertips. Hundreds were always newer, had spent less time in people's hands. Regardless, the protocol was, once the rubber bands were off, take out seven bills and hope that was enough. Otherwise, we would have to repeat the whole undertaking the next day.

In fact, Mami, I always took eight and kept one for myself. I felt that the satisfaction of you not being in trouble was not enough to justify my terror. So skimming a little extra was a way to make it worth it.

The reason it was terrifying, of course, was that it could go wrong. Sometimes Dad would snort hard, like he was stirring, while I was still under the bed. If you didn't move from your spot by the door, it meant that everything was ok, he was just turning over, and I could wait it out. A few times, though, he actually woke up, and then we were in trouble. If Dad had ever found me under his bed with his money, he would have killed me! Maybe literally.

One time he even got up and sat on the side of the bed. I could see his legs. When this happened, I remember, oh Mami, you were just brilliant. Quickly, you walked in the door and told him you needed money for something. You knew he would refuse, but that refusal gave him a reason not to reach down and check his money, and the ensuing loud conversation gave me cover to quickly put the rubber bands back on the wad and the wad back in the pocket. Then I just had to stay still and wait until he fell back to sleep.

Once I had taken the money, then I had to slide backwards to the door without hitting the bed legs. Once I was close enough, you would just grab my leg and pull me the rest of the way. I would hand over the bills, and you would hug me, hard. I loved when you did that. It made me feel as if I was important in your life, which was not always the case. You would kiss me on my cheeks and smile and sometimes cry. "We are a good team," you would say.

In summer, I remember, it was a little safer, because you could put on the AC to give me sonic cover. Which—by the way—why did we have an AC unit? We were poor! At most, the other families in the government housing might have invested in a patio or a fence, and there we were with a fucking AC! I guess that is where the money went: on things we didn't need, things that made you feel better than everyone else. I can relate to that, Mami. So, so much!

ᔕ

The other person you had me running operations on was Aunt Anita. I don't feel like I ever tricked her, though, because I loved her. I truly enjoyed my time with her, so the things I had to do at your request don't make me feel as terrible as they might. They really weren't terrible, Mami, but they could be interpreted that way by others.

To me, Aunt Anita always signified that it was possible to make it in life. She had married a good man, a tenant farmer who worked hard and saved up enough to buy the land, and then went on to make what seemed to us like a lot of money. They loved each other, though admittedly, out there in the country, there wasn't exactly anyone else to love. Anita was not able to have children, but unlike most women I knew, she didn't appear to give a shit about it. She was focused on her own happiness. When her man died, her happiness just shifted. She turned from enjoying life on a farm to moving to the city to be closer to her mother (that bitch Nonna Emma) and her sister (Aunt Maria). And she also decided, as she put it, to enjoy the children of others without having any responsibilities for them.

That decision is why, when she opened the door of one of the many empty rooms off the long corridor in Nonna Emma's house and walked in on Ali fucking me in front of the mirror on the door of the big armoire, and also over another mirror he had placed on the floor in order to see his dick entering my body (he was very into this, Mami! I could never understand it, but somehow it was hot), she simply closed the door and walked away.

I don't think Anita thought what she saw was hot. I am sure she did not agree with it or favor it. But I also don't think she thought she should care about it or get involved. I was not her child, and it was not her problem, so she closed the door, and when I came out later, we continued as if nothing had happened. I went into the kitchen, and she asked me if I wanted to make pizza with her. Pizza from scratch! My favorite! Though I did notice that she pointedly asked me to very carefully wash my hands before kneading the dough. She avoided not only drama, but also germs!

Although she disliked getting involved in other people's shit, I think Anita truly enjoyed me. I know I had a lot of fun hanging out with her. She would come over to Nonna Emma's late in the morning to help make lunch and hang out. She'd stay until about 7 pm, then return to the house she had bought close by, where she could have her privacy. But if I happened to be at Nonna Emma's, she would usually invite me to spend the night in her house. I always said yes, and of course there was no need to ask permission—neither you nor Dad would notice I was gone. At her house, she would tell me stories and make me hot chocolate. Sometimes we would have some brandy before bed. I kept doing this, I think, until I was about 16, when my nights started to be occupied going to bars with Juan Pablo and hunting dick instead.

Anita was smart, and funny, and not someone to fuck with. But I was smarter. And you knew that, Mami. I could trigger the nights she would invite me to go sleep over. I knew how to do that. All it took was some expression of interest in her life and her experiences, or a simple question about her husband. I swear, Mami, I enjoyed asking these questions. It wasn't a sneaky terrible thing. I enjoyed paying attention to her, knowing that my ear was of use to someone. And I loved that I was making Dad happy by being interested in her, something I wasn't able to do often. So I would go to Anita's regularly, and usually without an ulterior motive. But sometimes those visits were requested by you.

I wish I could remember who your contact was at the bank, the one who would call you. You hated receiving their calls. Whenever they rang, we had to act. No time for bullshit—it meant immediate business.

Somehow, you always managed to get the bank to lend you money. Often, you were paying back several loans at once.

I still don't understand why they lent to you, but something I do know is that banks are evil. Maybe that was where all your money went: on paying interest that would never end. Interest over interest, all going to the institutions where your employers worked, collecting hefty salaries that allowed them to employ you to iron their nice white shirts so you could get more money to pay the bank.

But someone in that evil institution was your friend, I guess, because they would tell you exactly the days when the letters to your guarantor were going out—that guarantor being Anita. Anita was cautious with her money, but also saw your humanity. I think she saw you as being like her, alone in the world. She knew that even if her brother was married to you, it meant nothing. In actuality, like her, you were manless, a lone woman fighting to stay alive. So she always signed on your loan applications, reassuring the bank it had someone to go to in case you didn't pay. Perhaps she also did this because she knew that, also like her, you always found a way to come out of anything. You would always make it. What she didn't know was that I was a fundamental part of that.

"Alejandro," you would say, "your aunt Anita will receive a letter from the bank tomorrow morning. The postman will deliver it as always, around 10 am. It is important that you intercept it. She cannot get her hands on that letter, or we will be in a lot of trouble. I need some extra time to pay this month, but Anita cannot know I am late. You know what needs to be done."

I did know what needed to be done. This was another exhausting operation. It was an extraction, much like the extraction of money from Dad's pocket, but with the difference that, whereas Dad was asleep, Anita was very much awake. Not only awake, but extremely aware of her surroundings. She told me once that as a woman without a man, she always had to worry about others trying to fuck her over, especially with money, as she had it and she was firm about keeping it.

Anita always got up early. She would attend to her plants, which always seemed to struggle despite her care and attention. Her sister Maria always had beautiful plants, even though she rarely, if ever, watered or tended to them. Anita hated that her sister had beautiful plants and she didn't. She also hated that her sister was tall and skinny and she wasn't. Possibly the two were connected.

Once she had seen to the vegetation, around 9 am, she would wake me up with tea and toast with butter, and we would chat about what we were going to do today. As I didn't have class until the afternoon, I would stay with her until she left, around 10 or 10:30 am. Which was exactly the time the mail usually came. Which was problem number one.

If the mailman was coming up the street at the same time Anita left, he would give her the mail in person, putting it into her very hands. That would have been a disaster. Unretractable. So it was important to ensure she didn't leave until the mail was in the box and I had time to get to it. My first task was therefore to create a distraction to make sure she stepped out later than usual.

The solution was easy. The plants! If I complimented the plants—especially if I observed certain ones getting prettier than the same ones Maria had—Anita would get very excited and spend time with me wandering around the plants, cleaning them or talking to them, letting them know we were very happy they were blossoming. As we did this, the trick was to maneuver our progress in such a way as to keep Anita's back to the street. As long as we were in the garden but looking towards the house, she would not see the mailman passing. I would see him, but she would not. Once he was safely gone, I would casually comment that the mailman had passed, but that he had left nothing. Then, when we were leaving, as she was locking the house, I would take all the letters from the mailbox, both the one I was after and any others. The others I could replace in the mailbox the next day, early, before the mailman came. The one from the bank, detailing your failure to pay on time, Mami, I would give to you.

Again, you would hug me so hard when I gave you the letters! I wish you could have also hugged me that hard when I was giving you nothing, but I do understand that doesn't mean you didn't love me. It just means you loved me more when I helped you. That is something your friends will never understand, because you always showed them love, even when they were terrible to you. Even when they talked shit about me, it was so important to you to make them happy.

﹏

It feels like I am scraping around looking for good memories to make up for all the things that were really fucked up about our relationship. Maybe I am. But all those terrible things were also showered with the longest, slowest, and most steady rain of loving drops. And that love did not come from the things we did for each other. I didn't feel love for you because of anything you specifically did for me. There weren't really many things you did for me that justified that love. It was just there.

We had to find ways to love each other in the middle of so much shame. I was a heavy rock to carry in your bag, and your bag was so full of other rocks that you just really didn't need one more with my name on it. I saw in your eyes so many times the wish that I was not your child. I saw your eyes broadcasting to me and to the world that life would be better if I could only be there in another capacity, not as your son. You always threw a cape over my actions for the sake of other people. You were compelled to minimize everything I did, looked like, or sounded like that made me seem queer.

And the reciprocity was perfectly even. I too had so many rocks in my bag that I wished at times you were not my mother. It felt impossible to be your child. I imagined you were a friend, someone I knew and liked, someone I could talk to and laugh with. I wanted you to exist as a woman bicycling her way through life, but not my mother. My guess is that most people wish the same. Or perhaps it is only me. But I know that, as often as you felt ashamed of me, I also felt ashamed of you, Mami.

Economics didn't help. Fucking poverty didn't make it any easier. I remember Helena asking me, about her parents, "Why did they have me? They don't have enough money to care for me. Why? Why?" She would even wish her parents dead. I never went that far, but I too always felt that I didn't belong in the poverty you had brought me into. Like, sure, I was happy we got public housing and an actual bathroom where I could take a shit on a fucking toilet instead of squatting in an outhouse. But for all that was better, it still never felt like the hand of cards I should have been dealt. I felt so strongly I deserved more that most of the time I couldn't even enjoy the luxury of flushing the toilet.

Moving to that low-income neighborhood was supposed to be our salvation, but it came with all the terribleness one could think of. Don't tell me you didn't realize that, because I know you did. Everything was worse, just in a better house. My feet may have preferred a mosaic tile floor to the bare ground, but that helped me develop that hip snap you hated so much. Having neighbors around instead of the isolation of a rat-infested hut made you realize that other people were also seeing the way I moved my hips, and they talked about it. And then school: all those terrible kids and teachers, all those terrible people in general!

These days, Mami, I work on what Americans call *social justice issues*. And I learned a word: *Inequality*. When I first heard someone use it, I had to Google what it meant, but as soon as I did, it made so much sense. I think *inequality* was one of the first overwhelming feelings I ever had, along with *alienation* (like when I realized I was an alien) and *possessiveness* (like when I watched Ali playing soccer and said to myself he was mine—not to keep or show around, but still mine).

I never had a problem being poor at Grandma's house. It was so isolated that it put me out of touch with money and people who had it, so there was poverty but no inequality. But in Galvez, at home, our house—the better house, the one with the bathroom, which was technically much fancier than Grandma's house—was still a poor person's house. It sat in juxtaposition to the pretty houses, the ones that didn't look all the same. And I felt it. I felt poor, and it was not an acceptable feeling.

Does this make me a conceited, egotistical little bitch? Of course it does! But why lie to you? I thought I deserved better, and you did not provide that, and I blamed you for it. I blamed you because I got a losing draw in the parent lottery.

～

It is a very Argentinian way to make decisions, through lotteries. Remember the lottery to decide who would be drafted into the military? They ran one every year, and all the seventeen-year-old boys in the area, including faggots like me, had to enter it. The way it worked was that there was a local radio broadcast. They would read out all the names of all the kids in the order they were drawn. It was so fucking scary! Especially because of all the rumors that spread about what military training was like.

By that time, I had already told you explicitly I was a faggot. I wasn't able, yet, to explain that "faggot" was an approximation, the only word I had for what I really felt, but I told you it was what I was. And so we were both very afraid: if I was drafted, how was I going to survive?

A few days before the draw, I saw Doña Marchesi in the street, and she smiled at me! A very suspicious move! Why, I asked myself, is she smiling? She looked me in the eyes. By that time, almost an adult, I was taller and less scared of her sharp tongue. I had developed a sharp one of my own. So I thought,

Bring it, bitch, and I stared back. Then she came over, still smiling, and said: "Are you ready for the draft? The army is where boys become men, and some boys need more help with that than others. I am praying the right ones come up in the lottery."

I had thought I was prepared for whatever she had to throw at me, but this caught me off-guard, without a riposte. I hesitated, like a boxer putting their arms up after a jab has hurt them. She saw the opening, and advanced: "I am a nurse, you know, I don't just deliver babies into the world. Being a nurse is almost like being a doctor. And as a nurse, I know all about what happens when the draftees get to the base. They ask everyone to strip. They form a line of hundreds of young boys, stark naked, and they watch how they look at each other."

She was winning! Fuck! Like an idiot, I stood there, too stunned to dodge or hit back as she readied her final assault. "Then they ask you to turn around and squat, push your ass up and separate your cheeks with your hands, and they come along one by one and look at your hole, and trust me! They know! They know whose asshole has been used in an ungodly way! If they find one with a loose asshole, the humiliation is endless. If you think they let you go right away, you are dreaming!" Remorselessly, she pressed her advantage. "Days of humiliation go by before these sodomites are sent home, and as a final step, to record their terrible findings, they sign in red on your ID card in the box for 'military service completion,' so that for the rest of your life everyone will know what you are, and you can never escape it."

This was vicious. Our confrontation had gone from traditional boxing, Queensberry rules, to a street fight. I was on the floor, unable to get up. Doña Marchesi decided to kick me while I was down. She looked at me, still smiling, and asked, "What is going to be? What color will the signature on your ID be, Alejandro?"

And then—I swear, if I believed in God I would say God helped me, because—I had an inspiration. "Ask your son, Doña," I said. "He will be able to give you that answer better than me."

She looked lost. Her son? Was he fucking me? He actually wasn't, he didn't have the balls for it, but I had planted the doubt. She brought her hands up to her hair, patted down her freshly permed curls to cover her confusion, then finally screamed, "You will get what's coming!" and left in a hurry. I am sure she went home to interrogate her son as to whether he was fucking the faggot.

But she had rattled me, all the same. Was what she said true? Was it really going to happen? I wanted to ask you about it. "Will I have to show my hole?" I wanted to scream to you. "Because, Mami, it is ripped! I get so much dick!" But I couldn't, of course—we were cool by then, but not that cool. I do, though, remember you looking at me with care and fear as we waited for the radio broadcast to start, holding hands.

The way the draw worked: They started naming the seventeen-year-old boys in the city, beginning from about 1000, all the way down to zero. If your name was mentioned before 700, you were screwed. From 700 to 500, you were still at risk. 500 down, you were safe.

I guess the universe chose not to play with my feelings, because at 856, there it was: "Gentili, Alejandro." I was going. You held me and we cried, and I felt so loved by you—not as a friend, or as a good person who loves others, but as a mother. A rare instance in our relationship.

∾

Why was it so rare? So hard? For a long time I blamed my queerness, but as I *am* queerness, Mami, as I *am* transness, it always comes back to blaming myself. As if I didn't or couldn't change myself enough to get your love.

Or else I think, if it was not something wrong with *me*, maybe it was something wrong with *you*. It is sometimes hard to resist the idea that you just didn't have it in you to love me. Maybe children, for you, were just a way to get out of poverty. Maybe when you decided to have us, you were hypnotized by the rainbows Dad sold you and thought that we were your ticket to a place better than Grandma's mud house in San Martin, without knowing that it would only be another mud house just like that one, maybe a bit bigger, and without anyone to love you in it. If that is so, Mami, it is okay.

Your first attempt at having a child, you always told me, failed. Well, I have to confess, I have known for a long time it was not just a failure: It was an abortion. One day when I was about seven years old, Nonna Emma took me into her room and opened a drawer of her dresser. Inside it was a wooden box. I had seen it before while sniffing around looking for secrets, but it was locked. I had always wondered what was in it, so when she took it out and sat on the bed and invited me to sit next to her, I was overcome with curiosity.

She took a small key from her pocket and unlocked it. It contained a gun. A silver gun. Very feminine, I thought, since it was very small. I was scared. Nonna Emma was clearly one of the worst people I knew, and it seemed to me she was absolutely capable of killing me and saying that I was playing with her firearm. But then she took the gun out and carefully laid it aside, and I realized something worse was coming. It would have been better if she had pointed the gun at me.

Beneath the gun were some papers. Emma took out a bundle of letters carefully tied with a lace ribbon. She slowly untied it. My heart was pumping hard. She took one letter out and opened it. I could see it was old, yellowed. She unfolded it, handed it to me, and asked me to read a specific paragraph.

"Dear Tito," it said, "I am way too late with my period. This is real. I am sure I am pregnant."

Shit. This was your handwriting. The first thought that came to me was, *disgrace!* You got married pregnant! But then I recalled all those beautiful pictures you loved to show of your wedding day, with Dad holding your extremely small waist. Those told a different story.

When I looked up, Emma already had another letter in her hand. She gracefully opened it and pointed to a line: "It is done. They took it from my body. Thank you for sending the money for the procedure."

Nonna was not just evil, she was calculating. She was the kind of person who tells a young child that their mother had an abortion as part of a plan to peel their loyalty away from her. But this move did not work out as she expected. I saw what she was doing. The nerve of her to think she could just manipulate me like that! Plus, I was already well aware (for some reason) of what an abortion was. Probably Helena had told me about it. I looked at her, Mami, and I told her: "I'm glad. Being number two is hard enough. I wouldn't want to be number three."

Emma shut the box top soundly and hard, looked at me, whispered, "You are just like her," and left.

What had she expected? That I was going to leave you and come to live with her like Claudio had?

Claudio was her pride. I saw her love him and adore him and go out of her way to conceal his bullshit. I saw her help him care about nothing and nobody. I saw her ironing his impeccable white shirts to perfection so he could go out with his richer-than-us friends with her money and come back drunk at all hours of the morning. I saw Emma and Maria having to carry him up to bed, trying to make sure he threw up anywhere but on that perfect shirt, so they would not have such a hard time washing it again. I saw them do all this just so he could do the same thing the next night with the same results, like a loop. And they did it with a joy that I will never know the reason for.

Was it that they needed to be dedicated to someone, a man, and he was the one they had? Did they see him as an extension of Papi, whom they had lost to you, Mami, irrevocably? Even if he left you, he wouldn't have come back to them; he would have replaced you with Inés, and they hated her too. I think they would have hated anyone who took Papi away from them. A story doesn't get any more Argentinian than that: A whore takes Mom's child away, ruining her life and leaving her empty.

I think that Claudio filled that void. He was their new son and brother. Of course, it didn't hurt that they were also taking him away from you. Letting you know that your healthy womb could get you Dad, but that you would have to have him without the family money, and that the child you produced in exchange for that never-realized illusion of wealth was also theirs. That was your punishment for taking the man of the family.

I think that, like I did, Claudio hated being so poor. He, as I did, hated having to warm water in a galvanized metal basin to "shower" in the same room where we cooked and slept. So with Nonna Emma, he saw an opportunity. He saw an actual shower coming from above his head in an actual bathroom with a sink and a toilet. He chose to walk on wood surfaces while we walked on dirt. Even after we moved to the government house, it was still much better for him to live with Nonna. He had no restrictions there. I mean, I didn't either, since that would have been too motherly for you. Rules? Ha! But the ruleslessness was different for him because it came without the poverty I breathed every day. It came with new shoes and change in his pockets and not having to steal from anybody.

ဟ

I had to take a couple of weeks away from this letter, Mami. I got depressed. I am not sure if *depressed* is the right term. Depression, I have been told, is a chemical imbalance, and I don't think that is my situation. Now, knowing about depression, I am able to see how sick you were. I never understood why you took pills to feel better, I never understood what they were doing for you, but it makes sense now. You were really depressed. Whereas I am just sad. It is hard to write to you and realize that I will not be writing a happy letter. It is hard to admit to myself that to find happiness in the history of our relationship, I have to make an effort. I have also been writing to other people, and that also has been difficult, but not as difficult as writing to you.

But it is not that we had no happiness in our relationship. As I keep writing this letter, your face keeps coming back into my mind. So peaceful and beautiful. I wonder if people ever told you that you were beautiful. Every time I think of you I can picture your face. Mostly in the kitchen, with the windows behind you and the sun coming through, hitting the side of your beautiful bronzed skin. You would catch me looking at you and move your head towards me and smile.

That smile was full of love. I felt you cherish me. I felt your love, Mami. Like the air, there although you can't touch it. So, when I talk about all the things you did that I believe were not right, I am not saying you didn't love me. I am saying sometimes people who love us don't know how to treat us right. I have had many of those in my life, I suppose because I was used to it and let it happen.

Last week I went to get a chair massage at the mall close to the house where I live now with Peter, my boyfriend. I have a boyfriend, Mami! Oh, God, you would love him. And he would have so much fun with you! When I got there, there was only one massage therapist available. He smiled at me and gestured for me to sit in his chair. But then, as the massage went on, he took my hand and rubbed it on his dick. I was disgusted as I felt his dick go from flaccidity to full hardness, but I didn't move or resist. I let him use a part of my body for his pleasure, and I even paid him for it. I came home more exhausted and tense than when I left. As soon as I crossed the front door and felt secure, I started feeling nauseated, and I ran to the bathroom and threw up bile.

Peter got worried, and I lied and said that I must have eaten something too heavy. But as I lied, I also made the connection to how violently ill you would sometimes get, apparently for no reason. The doctors blamed it on your gallbladder, but then they removed it, and you only got worse. Now I think your sickness may just have been your body being unable to contain all the frustrations you were living with: Dad, poverty, me.

I thought about how it felt as I put my hair in a quick ponytail to keep it away from the bile cascading from my lips. I couldn't help but wonder if this feeling was something you were familiar with: the feeling of being touched, being used, and not being able to yell or stop it.

This is the hard part, Mami. This is the whole reason I am writing this letter. I can't hide it anymore. Like vomit, it needs to come out of me.

I know if I had ever attempted this face to face, you would have found a way to run away from it. This is the benefit of a letter. I just get to tell you what I need,

and we can't run. As much as I want to think what I am about to say would have surprised you, I know it wouldn't have. Mami, I know you knew. To say this is not to say you are responsible for what he did or to blame you in any way. I am not looking to lay any guilt on you beyond whatever you already carry. But we can't keep acting as if it didn't happen, Mami.

It was a cold Sunday, and unusually, Miguel's wife had gone away from home and taken the children with her. She tasked Miguel with minding her grocery store, which was next to their house. You needed butter for a cake. I think it was your friend Lidia's birthday on Monday, and you wanted to have a cake ready for her. So you sent me to get it.

I can imagine how it must have seemed from Miguel's perspective. Who would have thought that the most dreaded chore in his life, minding his wife's business, would bring him, on a platter, the sweetest of compensations: me, already groomed and ready to do as he pleased? And, by a stroke of extreme luck, with nobody else in the store.

He quickly told me to get out and, once outside, without looking suspicious, go into their house and wait for him. I only waited a couple minutes before he came in. He immediately went down on his knees and kissed me. He said, "My little girl, what a treat! You do know that you will always be my girl, right?" I told him that I knew that. Then he took me to the bedroom and pulled out his smelly, hooded dick and asked me to suck it, as always, "like a lollipop."

Sometimes, Mami, I almost preferred the pain of him fucking me to the taste of urine stuck in between the head and the skin of his cock, but I sucked it all the same. I sucked it just so I could keep listening to his deep voice calling me "my girl." It didn't take long that day. I guess he was afraid his family would come back at any moment, so he let himself come quickly. Then he squatted to look me in the eyes. As always, I got distracted looking at his skin tags and how they proliferated in the region of his neck. He clenched his fingers, leaving the index finger semi-extended, put it right under my chin to redirect my eyes to his, and told me, "You know nobody loves you and cares for you as I do, right?" I nodded yes, and he let me go. But as I was about to open the front door, he reminded me to not forget my coya hat with pom-poms hanging from the ear coverings.

Maybe if I had left the hat behind, I would have missed you turning around the corner to see me coming out of the house. Not the store, the house. You froze and moved your eyes from me to him, coming out just behind me. For a couple seconds that felt like hours, none of us moved.

I could see your eyes becoming glazed, as if you were suffering from a short-lived cataract. I felt as if the world would end. I knew I would be unable to find a way to explain to you what was happening.

But as it turned out, no questions were exchanged. Only he spoke. Looking peacefully at your blurry eyes, he said: "I'm afraid we don't have butter at the store, or at home . . . " You simply took my hand and pulled me towards you and started walking back home.

As we crossed the park, I pulled back to stop you. Looking at you, I said: "Mami . . . "

You pressed my hand with your big hand and said, "I know, my baby, I know." And then you shushed me with your finger over my lip. "Don't worry, I can use oil instead," you said. "We will be just fine!" Then we continued walking back home.

I can't stop crying, Mami, as I write this right now. Not because of what was happening to me at that moment, but because I wish I could have asked you: What happened to you that made you navigate all of this as if it was normal? I wish I could have had an adult conversation with you, as friends, but something we did a lot was to use our mother-and-child status to avoid hard topics.

It is important to repeat, I am not putting any blame on you for your inaction. I know I was not good to you either, in many ways. I know none of the things we did to each other were intentional. They just were. I would even venture that most of the harm we caused to each other came from good intentions. But of course we know where those lead.

～

I know, for instance, that you had the best intentions when you found a way to send me to the lyceum to study music, using your connections as a cleaning lady there. But you never consulted me about it. I believe you thought, *this child is so delicate that the best thing I can do is to help him get a career in the arts*. But I was terrible at music. Yes, I loved it. I loved knowing about history and being able to appreciate a baroque early toccata, but it should have been clear even to you that I lacked musical talent. I sucked at guitar, flute (although I was already great at blowing), and piano. And I sucked at them because I hated studying them! All the girls in the Lyceum could study for hours, but I had things to do. It was hard to dedicate time to practice when I had to find time to be me, Mami! And being me was more important than Mozart.

Plus, being the only poor boy in the middle of all those rich girls was terrible. They made sure to remind me I was not one of them. Though maybe I am being bitchy now, because many of them were nice. Actually, one of them became one of my best friends in the world: my sister Norma. Every time I say anything bad about you to her, she gets really upset with me. I tell her: "You only knew her as the cleaning lady at the art school. I lived with her."

Maybe it wasn't the rich girls. Maybe it was me. I hated being the child of the cleaning lady. It was just hard, you know? "Call your mom, I spilled water on the table!" "Tell your mom the bathroom needs toilet paper!" I know you were trying to help, but like so many things you did to help me, it was an awful experience.

That resentment was why, when Susana Jiminez told me about her plan to engage in shoplifting in order to obtain for our poor selves the same kind of fancy clothes the girls at the Lyceum wore, I did not hesitate. Why not me? I wanted to feel the same fabrics on my skin! And, I told myself, if everything goes to shit, I can take it. I will be fine. I want to enjoy a bit of luxury even if I have to pay for it with shame later. What do I have to lose? Even in the worst-case scenario, I get a few days of walking in the same shoes as all those rich piano-player hoes!

Of course, we got caught. There was a small scandal. Everyone at school looked at me weird for a week, then moved on to the next piece of gossip, but it was not a big deal to me. But for you it was. You beat me really badly. I remember you did it with a jean jacket I had stolen from this boutique in Rivadavia Street. You yelled: "You want a jean jacket? Here it is!" Then you hit me hard as many times as you could before you became too tired and out of breath. All the time you were hitting me, you cried and cried. I remember meeting Juan Pablo afterwards. He helped me put Vaseline on all the bruises, exact replicas of the buttons on the jacket.

ᔓ

I think you were so angry, Mami, because you were trying to protect me. Like I say, good intentions. But in some way you must have succeeded because I am still here, which we cannot say for everyone. Do you remember "El Mudo Blanco"? What a beautiful butterfly! He represented everything I wanted to be and everything I didn't at the same time.

They called him mute, but he was able to produce sounds, so I guess he was just deaf, and as he couldn't talk in a way that people could understand, he simply remained silent most of the time. I never interacted with him, but I observed him closely. I observed him as you observe a spider, carefully, focused and at a distance, watching while making sure they are not feeling watched.

I believe he was about 10 years older than me and unimaginably rebellious and free, in a way I dreamt of but knew I could not replicate. He was it! He was the faggot who lived with no concern for Galvez's opinions. Maybe because he could not hear what they whispered about him, or even the things people would yell at him as he walked, moving his hips as I knew I could also move them, as I had to stop myself from moving them. Defiant, uncaring, self-centered, he was the star of his own movie and nothing else, it seemed, mattered to him. I had my movie, too, but he *lived* in his. Mine was just a roll of celluloid; his was a reality! I wanted to be like him, but I just couldn't. I remember walking along with you, holding hands, and if we saw him, you would pull my hand, making a statement that something abnormal was happening, telling me to keep away, to not go closer, to not be like that. And then one day, something happened which seemed to vindicate your warnings.

Juan Pablo came to our house, which he never did, because you had made it very clear he was not welcome. Doña Presenta was equally clear that I was not allowed at his house either.

So I knew something important was happening. He stood in the street and asked for me. He was shaking. He was not crying, but he looked like he was about to start. He said we should go to the eucalyptus forest so we could talk, and he ran off. I ran after him, across the little twin parks on the corner, past the empty house Alemana used to live in, to the corner of the main road, where he stopped to avoid a speeding car. I caught him. I took his hand and he looked at me and began crying. "It is bad," he said.

I wanted to ask him what was happening, but I knew he needed to be in a safe place, so I took a big breath and, as the car passed, started running again, this time holding his hand. We passed the old hospital where Doña Marchesi kept watch. Right around the corner, where the town abruptly ended, the majestic eucalyptus forest stood, making the noise of millions of leaves hitting each other as the wind blew, releasing the most amazing smell.

We ran inside and moved fast between the trees until we made it to the point that, somehow, we considered the middle of the forest. We knew that place better than our own homes. It was a sacred place of our sisterhood. At that time, the city was proposing to log it, and we were very worried. Without it, we would have nowhere private. Now it is gone, of course. But then it still offered us a refuge.

We sat on the floor. It was so soft. The dead leaves created a bouncy cushion. Juan Pablo held my hand and told me: "They are hunting us."

Everything stopped. The trees stopped rustling, the smell went away, the cushion disappeared. An empty feeling occupied my whole chest. There was no need to define "us." I knew it was "us fags." I knew it was me and him.

"They killed El Mudo Blanco," he said. Even my heart stopped. It was like it took a break from pumping. As I am writing to you now, Mami, I can feel the same sensation I experienced then. A feeling like a light that comes right from my silent heart, between my big boobs, and spreads out all over my body, into my extremities. "How?" I asked. "When? Where?"

Juan Pablo started crying in a much more intense way. Mucus came out of his nose.

He said, "Do you know the old abandoned railroad sheds?" I nodded *yes*, and he said, "By the big elm?"

"Yes," I said.

"I heard someone, or most likely two people, or more, took him there. I think he went there to meet someone to fuck, but in reality they wanted not to fuck him but to kill him. And whoever that person was was successful with their plan. They strangled him and turned him on his stomach and raped him with a branch of the same elm that saw the whole murder, and they left him there. That is going to be us," he said. "We are going to be next."

I was paralyzed. We both were. We sat there for I don't know how long, making promises to each other, like that we would not play alone anymore, and that we would not go alone to meet any strangers to fuck, anywhere. I put my arm around his shoulders and told him, "It will not be me and it will not be us, Juan. We will leave this town soon; I promise you, we will not die here. Not here and not like that." It was usually Juan who gave me courage and was more assertive, but that day it was me.

As I walked home, I wondered if you would know what had happened. I knew how quickly news traveled in a little town. And you did. You were, unlike ever before, actually waiting for me and ready to talk. You sat me down and ran your hands through my hair and proceeded to tell me that you were not intending to ever cry for me as Mudo's mother must be crying for him, that you would not be crying for your son after they found him dead and impaled, that you would not let what happened to him happen to us.

It was like a monologue. I did not get many words in. It felt as if there was no space for them. It was just you, telling me for once how things would go and even, for once, explaining the reasons for what you were about to do. It was so scary hearing you sound like a mother.

"We are going to go to the hair salon and we are going to cut your hair very short," you told me. "You will not complain or cry. You will not try to trick me as you do to gain time until I forget. Your hair empowers you to act feminine. You keep swinging it and moving it like the models do. We can't have that! It's not that I don't like your hair. Your hair is beautiful, my child. Especially if you look at mine, so nappy and dry. You have your dad's hair. I guess you got something good from that man after all. But it has to go.

"You may see me as wanting to hurt you with this, and I understand, but hurting you is not my intention, my love. I just want you to live. And if you don't live, I want you to die in an accident. I want you to have a terrible illness that is out of our control. I want to feel as if there is nothing that I can do to stop it from happening. I want people to know that this is not something I could have prevented. But in reality, I want you to live, and that is not going to happen if you keep acting like a girl." I started to cry, and you did, too. "This is to help you get through your time in this little town so you can go and do as you want, but the only way to do that is to live, and it doesn't look like you will make it otherwise."

Juan Pablo always tells me that in his view, you couldn't wait for me to go away. This may sound terrible, but I think you knew that we could not relate civilly as long as we were in the same house or even in the same city, and that is not totally your fault. I have to own that. I was not a good daughter, either, and it makes sense that after so many years of fighting, disliking each other, being ashamed of each other, scamming and lying to each other, we found a way to be best friends when I was able to find distance.

I was a mess, Mami. My whole manipulative self wants to say I was a mess "of a child," to make a pitch for sympathy and exculpation, since children do crazy shit and can't be held responsible, but the truth is, even as a child, most of my shitty actions were very well thought out. It was just that I took a different lesson from what happened to Mudo than you did.

See, Mami, I am taking responsibility. So rare in our family.

It was the same lesson I applied when Susana Jimenez invited me to go shoplifting. I knew it was dangerous. It was very clear to me that this adventure was not going to be endlessly sustainable and that there would eventually be consequences. Still, I made the decision to do it. I thought, *This is going to end badly, but I still want to have nice clothes for once*. This way of thinking has followed me throughout my life: *Let's steal this client's money* or *Let me try to shoot seven bags of heroin at once*. They are the same calculation. *Let me do it*, I always thought; *I may get murdered tonight, so it doesn't matter*. I had learned to evaluate risk on a whole other level than you and most of the people I knew.

Also, I couldn't help but think, Mami, how were these clothes different from the money we took from Papi? Now I see the answer was simple: it was that others knew about it. For you, what others said about us was more important, more dangerous than what we thought about ourselves, what we said about ourselves to ourselves. Maybe that was the reason you decided to let Miguel keep fucking me in the ass as a child. Maybe, for you, it was better not to risk being judged as a bad mother of a queer child who "wanted it." But you were keeping me safe from the wrong things.

I need to say this, Mami. It needs to be said, even if this letter ends up looking like a torrent of culpability. But the reason I need to say it so much is because it is only once I have said it that I can also say: I understand. For once, I am not going to judge you for your actions. I am not going to be one of *them*. When I moved away, our relationship got better, but now you are dead, and that is too far away. I want you to come back. I miss you more than anyone.

Cecilia

Delia

YOUR NECK.

I have a tendency towards what is called *synecdoche*. That is, I often associate people with specific parts of their bodies. Gorgeous hair, bad skin, crooked teeth, long arms, and so on. When I think of you, the first thing that comes to mind is your neck.

I hate your neck. You might expect I would hate your eyes (always judging) or your index finger (never shy to indicate the ones cast out of your circle of purity) or your mouth, with its outpourings of cruel verbiage (rarely overtly nasty, but always piercing, designed to hurt while ostensibly remaining within the boundaries of civility), but no. It is your neck I hate.

The turning of your neck was the first sign of your guillotine-operator enterprise going into motion. As a camera sees only where it turns and must be mounted on a tripod or a track, so your eyes moved, but only on your neck. Your neck is what drove your laser-focused righteousness-embracing scrutiny. I was always on the side of the ones your neck turned towards, the ones who then got the rest of your arsenal, the gestures, the narratives of our unworthiness. Oh the shade! Who the fuck gave you that power? You awful human being. What made you think you were born to rule?

You, as the midwife, were the first to hate me as I came out of my mother. Perhaps that is what gave you your conviction that you possessed a right to judge. For most of us children, you were the one who saw us for the first time, and so you felt you knew us. As we were born, your neck would turn your eyes upon us, and you foresaw our lives as they were bound to be. Nothing, in your books, could ever change what you saw—though in my case, whatever harsh judgements you made at my birth must have been confirmed by what your neck later allowed you to witness.

I can envision now, for instance, your perfectly calibrated veering neck making the exact movement required to catch me coming out of the eucalyptus forest on one side, and then carefully and with absolute precision twisting through a one-hundred-and-twenty-degree angle to bring into view, on the other side of the trees, the spot where Helena's husband was fighting the dead branch of a shrub that had stuck between the spokes of his competition-grade bicycle. He stupidly looked up, first at me making my escape, and then at you watching us both, at which point, in a slightly less stupid move, he whistled as if everything was normal.

You, with your inescapable neck, clearly knew it wasn't. As I looked back, I could see you tearing up. Were you asking your maker *why?* Why was someone like me breathing the same air as you? Why was I suffered to exist? But you needed me, darling.

Because I can also envision, once I had gone out of sight, once its work of directing your gaze towards my wicked actions was done, your neck returning to its usual perfect, straight alignment with the rest of your backbone—a movement expressive of holy resignation, of your confidence that your suffering would only bring you closer to God. I represented the world-

CECILIA GENTILI

ly terribleness that, if tolerated, would become an agony that could only illuminate your perfection. You needed me to be bad so you could feel good. I guess I have always been a bit of a people-pleaser, because I always seemed to try to give you exactly what you needed.

And so, Delia, I am going to tell you exactly what happened that day. I think you deserve the relief of knowing. I feel as if not fully knowing may be preventing you from going with a light heart to meet your God, in the maximal consciousness of your own righteousness. As I am trying to be a better person, I'm willing to help you take those final steps towards your salvation, so you can die sooner.

First, I can tell you that Helena's husband was not the first man who fucked me. Miguel, for one, started fucking me when I was just a child. For some reason, I think I am not breaking any news to you when I tell you this. I suspect you knew what he was doing, and that you think it was my fault, that it was me who provoked it, but if I am past anything, I am past thinking I bear any kind of responsibility for Miguel's twisted actions, so don't waste your time, darling, laying that shit on me. I will allow you plenty of opportunities to justifiably accuse me, but Miguel is not going to be one of them. I will not allow you or anybody else to even begin to suggest that was my fault. No.

Then there were others. Do you already know about them all? Alejandro fucked me as a teen and gave me a feeling of control. He would do anything and risk anything just to be with me. Here you can judge, feel free. Would you like another? Gabriela's stepdad went down on me. There I was just practicing, as I was with many others. That's another opportunity for you, Delia. Condemn it as you wish!

And then Helena's husband, which I know you do know about. He gave me a whole different feeling, a feeling of recompense. Not just validation of my gender or my capacity to enjoy sex, but a sense that I could take compensation from others, that it was ok for me to just take, that I could be ok with that. While he fucked me, all I thought was: "Here it is, Helena. Your trophy. I am taking it." Sex with Helena's man taught me that using what I had at hand to put myself a bit less on the bottom was okay. I never thought I wanted to keep him. Just *have* him. I didn't want to be like her. I just wanted to take from her.

Are you enjoying this, Delia, me confirming in writing all the worst things you could have whispered about me? In my defense, ever since her marriage, Helena had taken a turn to the awful side. Her unhappiness was mounting. She had put so much effort into getting this man, and she had succeeded, but none of the things she had aspired to were materializing as a result. Admittedly, he had given her a house of her own, at a sufficient distance from her violent father and her suffering mother and brother, but then she had to clean it. He had given her a ring, but the union could not be blessed by a priest, because he was separated and the "real" status of wifehood was already possessed by another woman, in relation to whom Helena would always have to feel inferior. He had given her a child, but now that child cried every night like a wolf on a full moon, non-stop, until she began to have the most wicked thoughts. I remember once I even found it necessary to step in and take the baby off her after she had slapped him violently. She was miserable as before, just in a different context, and meanwhile I had just started to enjoy life and be truly free, and she couldn't take it.

Being my "friend" made her aware of how things had changed. It was me getting pretty for the club now; it was me getting the attention of the cute boys; it was me going to sleep late and carefree, me making new friends while she didn't. I truly think she didn't mean to start hating me, but we had been so close for so long, she couldn't just be indifferent. My joy highlighted her misery, and she started being nasty to me.

And then Helena got pregnant a second time. As part of her campaign of nastiness, in order to underscore her ability to procreate and my lack thereof, she decided to ask me to be the godfather. Godfather! This was an especially hurtful request because it was such a gendered title, and I had told her already that I wished I was a woman. She was one of the first people I explicitly told I was more than a simple faggot. I remember she laughed and cupped her pussy with her hand and said, "How? How are you going to get one of these?" So she knew what she was asking. I told her I couldn't accept. I had plans for my life and the responsibility that an Argentinian godchild brings (that Catholic culture!) was not compatible with the kind of life I wanted to live. But she pressured me, she refused to take no for an answer, and eventually I gave in. I had already loved her for being horrible to me for so long, and I couldn't stop.

But I also looked for ways to strike back. And I found one. It was a couple of days before the ceremony where I held little Brenda in my arms as the priest poured a drip of holy water over her forehead (poor Brenda! I wish I could have been a better godmother to her. I wish I could have helped her when her mother died. But I wasn't and I didn't) that I had sex with Helena's husband. I needed to take something from her. I felt entitled to take it. I even almost felt entitled to let her know, although in the end I chickened out from that one. I wish I had told her. RE-CI-PRO-CI-TY. I wanted her to keep her hand cupping her pussy forever as she realized it meant nothing, that it was nothing special, and that her man would poke his dick into anything because he couldn't help it. I wanted to make her roll a little movie in her mind of all the times she was a bitch to me with no regrets, and I wanted her to know that I didn't have any, either.

Does this make me a bad person? Of course it does! I am not writing this letter to you, Delia, to justify my actions. I have not always been above painting myself as a victim, and trust me, I have gained some victories that way, but that is not what is happening here. It would have been lovely, at that time, to have been in a better place, to have been able to let it go and forgive Helena and forget it all, but that is not where I was, and I am not interested in concealing or downplaying the malice with which I acted. I am totally okay with it. I am merely illuminating you with the truth, to allow you to really put your hatred of me to work.

In fact, I feel, as I write this to you, something like I felt that day when I fucked Helena's husband, when I came out of the eucalyptus forest and saw your neck craned towards me and your eyes, yet again, giving me that terrible judgmental gaze that only you know how to give. Facing such a stare, I would usually have looked down and trembled in fear of what was about to come while also considering how to get back at you with some witty counterattack. I didn't. Instead, Delia, I took a big breath. For the first time ever, I was unafraid of you. You could think whatever you wanted about me, and you could tell everyone about my devilish spirit and dish as you liked about my evil nature. I would own it all and be happy. All the laughter at me wearing Mary's veil at the nativity, all the little comments about my weirdness, all the taunting and the mocking, every time you raised the pitch of your voice to repeat something I said while waving your hands to make fun of my feminine little self, it all seemed worth it.

I held my head high, and I looked back at you and waited. This time I would not be the one looking down first. As the stupid man who had just fucked me finally pulled himself together and got on his bike and rode away, whistling to cover his shame and desire, I continued to stand and look at you. I was telling you that this time, for once, I would not feel mortified; this time I would feel no guilt; you could not hurt me any more.

It felt good, darling, but it did not last long. In my life, it has been Delias everywhere. At school and at music school, next door and at the club. My clothes and my hair and the mascara I wore and the high pitch of my voice: every little thing was always under scrutiny. I realized you were just the first one, the one who was boldest with your hate, but that hate was everywhere, even if not always as dauntless as yours. It was subtle and sneaky at times; it even came indirectly through my mother and everyone else I cared about, whose lives were made just a bit more unbearable because I was in them. It came through everyone having to fight to explain why they were part of my life, to defend my existence as worthy. I wish I could say that that day, by the eucalyptus forest, when I met your gaze until you eventually blinked, and looked down, and left, was the last time I felt affected by you, but the reality is that even now, I still fear your judgement, and your sharp verdicts on my actions and life still haunt me.

I am putting this letter, Delia, in a book. I wonder if any of you in Galvez will read it. If you do, what will you all think? I know I am shaking the tree, challenging the fake reality where you all live at peace. So if they do read it, people are going to be very upset. But this is what I was always doing, just by existing: I was always challenging that perfect picture you all thought you had. This book isn't a book about my behavior. It is about unmasking the behavior of all those around me as a child.

I still think, Delia, that if I say it out loud, if I say the truth—that I was sexually abused consistently for years as a child—then you and those in your big ample corner are still going to whisper that I am either lying or that I was responsible for it. I believe this is what you did whisper, in fact, back when it was happening. And even if I know I am not responsible, I can't help but feel affected by this judgement. I wish I could say I am letting go of you, of all of you in Galvez, that I don't care what you think or say anymore, but I know this carefreeness is nothing but a wish or a temporary state. You still live in my head. I am writing to you to say you do win here, but also that that doesn't mean I have to lose. I am reexamining, these days, the idea of the winner.

I have realized that ABBA was wrong: The winner does not take it all. You might win, but I am taking something too, and guess what? you cannot recover it from me or take it away. I am taking the power to say out loud what happened. This power it is mine and only mine, to keep. Whoever is inconvenienced by it is, I know now, not as important as my need to say it. Does that make me a winner? Maybe not. But at fifty years of age, feeling that I am not a loser—feeling like my life has value too—is still winning.

And I am also going to say one more thing—and as I say this, I feel something changing in me—Fuck you, Delia.

I know I ought to say you are forgiven, but I won't. I still wish I could break your neck.

Cecilia

PS: Thanks for the heads-up about the military examination, it all happened exactly as you told me it would.

ACKNOWLEDGEMENTS

Thank you to my editors and publishers, Cat and Casey, for believing in my stories, and to all my friends, from Juan Pablo to Norma to the ones in this country, who have transcended to be family as I redefined it.

To the ones that get my crap, the drama and the laughs: Gogo, Lala, Cristina and Cyd.

About LittlePuss

LittlePuss Press is a feminist press run by two trans women, Cat Fitzpatrick and Casey Plett. We believe in printing on paper, intensive editing, and throwing lots of parties.

This book is set in Filosofia,
a font created in 1996 by Zuzana Licko,
drawing inspiration from the designs
of Giambattista Bodoni.